WILD AND HOLY

WILD AND HOLY

A JOURNEY THROUGH GRIEF, GUILT, AND GRACE IN ITALY

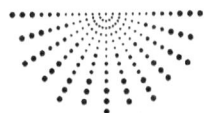

KAREN WYATT MD

For Larry, my intrepid, adventurous husband and steadfast travel companion—with me every step of this wild and holy journey of love and life. You make everything possible.

And for Italy, the Beautiful Country who opened her arms, held my sorrow, and returned me to myself.

"What I know about living is that the pain is never just ours. Every time I hurt I know the wound is an echo, so I keep listening for the moment the grief becomes a window, when I can see what I couldn't see before."

— ANDREA GIBSON

CONTENTS

AUTHOR'S NOTE

This is a memoir, drawn from memories, journal entries, and personal reflections from a grief pilgrimage through Italy. I've done my best to reconstruct the journey faithfully, but I recognize that memory is imperfect and that details may have shifted with time. Some names have been changed for privacy, and interpretations offered here are shaped by my own evolving spiritual perspective.

This story is not meant to be a guidebook or documentary account—it is a deeply personal exploration of grief, guilt, and grace through the lens of sacred travel and inner transformation. I also made use of AI tools for research, reflection, and organization during the writing process, but the stories and words are entirely my own.

While I am not Catholic and do not practice within any one religious tradition, I found deep spiritual resonance in the sacred spaces of Italy—many of which are churches. In these places, I encountered centuries of devotion, art, and human longing carved into stone and culture. My reflections are not theological or doctrinal, but contemplative and personal.

Many of the saints whose lives inspired me are steeped in myths and legends that are part of their spiritual legacy. I record those stories here because they were transformative for me at the time of this journey whether totally factual or not. These mystical teachers from the past transcended the religions that formed their foundations and share universal wisdom available for all of us.

My spiritual orientation is eclectic and contemplative, shaped by mystical traditions, nature, poetry, and lived experience. Throughout this journey I found inspiration not only in churches and saints, but also in ruins and olive trees, frescoes and fountains, street musicians and ancient stones ... as the soul speaks through many languages.

May you receive it with the same generosity of spirit.

INTRODUCTION

A RUINED TRIP TO ITALY

I sat motionless and numb in the waiting area of the international terminal where my flight to Rome would soon be taking off. Every fiber of my being was telling me not to go—the trip was ruined already and it would be a disaster. My heart was somewhere else and I couldn't seem to retrieve it.

This downward spiral of grief was familiar to me but I hadn't experienced it for years. I thought I was finished with grief but here it was again ... snatching my soul down to its underworld on the very day we were embarking on our second honeymoon.

I rehearsed what I would say to my husband when I turned to leave the airport: "I'm sorry—I'm just too broken right now to go on this trip."

"I can't do it."

"Please forgive me."

But when I raised my eyes to speak I saw the look of joy on his face—pure excited anticipation of our dream vacation, the second honeymoon we had looked forward to for years. I couldn't break his heart. I couldn't crush him under the grief that was crushing me. I didn't want to go, but I couldn't stay behind either. The choice had already been made by something deeper than will.. I *had* to go through the motions and make the best of it. The cost of canceling our shared dream was just too great.

This is the story of that ruined trip to Italy during the H1N1 flu pandemic ... of the unexpected event the morning of our departure that plunged me into a grief spiral ... of a journey I wanted to cancel but continued out of love ... of an unplanned pilgrimage through grief that ended up changing everything.

I didn't recognize what was happening while we were there—only in retrospect could I see that I had experienced an archetypal journey that required a descent into the depths of my own past grief before I could return with new wisdom. Joseph Campbell calls this the Hero's Journey and describes it as a universal pattern found in stories across centuries, cultures, and religions. But I have come to think of it as a "Healer's Journey": one that is required in order to walk beside others through the darkness of life and become the medicine necessary for healing.

This journey—which I now see more clearly after years of reflection—forms the framework for the book. First **The Departure**—a disruption in my ordinary world that forced me to leave it behind and undertake a journey to the unknown. Next **The Descent**—a process of entering into my inner depths and the pain of grief and guilt. Finally **The Return**—coming back home as a new person and the challenge of integrating new wisdom into my old life.

And that has turned out to be a lifelong journey, even though the pilgrimage described here took place on one two-week trip to

Italy. To this day I continue to cycle through the insights and lessons it taught me, ever-expanding in my understanding and wisdom.

This Healer's Journey took me to the underworld of my psyche where I had long ago sequestered the grief and guilt that were too painful to address after my father's suicide death. Within my Shadow I saw the archaeology of my old exiled grief, tangled with a lifetime of feeling responsible for the pain of the world, and believing I wasn't good enough to do anything about it.

Amazingly and somewhat miraculously all of this unfolded on a trip we had planned one year earlier as a romantic getaway. Though the itinerary for the trip remained the same as planned, the actual experience was totally different than anything I could have imagined.

Grief formed the lens through which I looked at Italy and shaped my awareness while I traveled from place to place, experiencing my own unique journey unlike any other ordinary tour through the country.

While this story follows the arc of the Healer's Journey, it unfolds in the book more like a mosaic: pieces of memory, ritual, history, and serendipity held together by the rough itinerary we had created for the trip a year in advance.

Some sections arose in sacred spaces or ancient ruins; others emerged from bus breakdowns, wrong turns, and quiet moments on trails and bridges. Interwoven throughout are reflections—small spirals of insight that have arisen over the years since that journey. Together, they form a map of grief and grace.

@

It was not random or inconsequential that Italy was the setting for this Healer's Journey. Looking back Italy was the perfect landscape for a pilgrimage of grief. The Romans believed that every location has what they named *genius loci* or "soul of place": a distinctive energy that permeates the culture, traditions, geography, art, and emotional resonance of a specific area.

This soul of place is tangible throughout Italy in its sacred cathedrals, buried ruins, bombed-out bridges, Roman roads, and crumbling arches. Italy is a land shaped by loss and grief throughout its long existence, but enduring with beauty, creativity and a passion for life that is vital and inspiring.

The depth of character is palpable when you are in Italy. You feel it in the air. You sense it in the physical structures you walk through, rising from the stones in the streets, hovering in the corners of cathedrals, permeating the taste of its slow food, and resounding in the passionate voices of music and art.

Italy was a safe container for me, the perfect backdrop for this Healer's Journey—this descent into my grief—because Italy carries grief out in the open. Italy is honest about her grief—she doesn't try to hide it, doesn't deny that it exists but wears it on display for everyone to see. Grief is tended and cherished and cared for as part of history and culture, and also as part of the connection to a universe that is built upon a cycle of life and death,

of order and disorder,

of darkness and light,

of joy and sorrow.

Italy is a place to weep and grieve unabashedly and Italy is also a place to celebrate the very miracle of being alive—to savor it, to feast and drink and sing and dance. Italy holds all of it in the open for us to participate and received me into her open arms on my journey.

When I didn't know what was happening or where I was going, Italy provided me with gentle nudges, inspirations, and intuition that kept me safe and held, but also guided and supported throughout the journey even though I didn't realize it at the time.

◎

The title of this book—*Wild and Holy*—emerged from the lived experience of grief as both unpredictable and sacred. It reflects the truth that grief, like love, cannot be managed or controlled.

Grief is wild in its nature: rising without warning, dashing our expectations, pulling us off-course from the map we thought we were following. And at the same time grief offers us an opportunity for spiritual growth that cannot be duplicated by any of the comfortable moments of life.

Wild grief cannot be contained—it floods us with emotion, spirals us into memory and longing, and breaks our hearts open again and again. This grief demands to be felt, heard, and honored and will wreak havoc if it is locked away and ignored.

Francis Weller wrote in *The Wild Edge of Sorrow*: "Grief reveals the undeniable reality of our bond with the world."

The wildness of our grief defines us as human, as part of the natural world. But, Weller goes on to say, grief also "offers a wild alchemy that transmutes suffering into fertile ground."

Grief is holy and reveals itself slowly—as grace, beauty, and meaning unearthed from pain. This holy aspect of grief is found in candlelit chapels and broken-open prayers, in moments of surrender, in the silence that follows sorrow. Holy grief is what we discover when we turn toward the pain instead of away; when we allow it to come to the surface instead of hiding it deep within.

To walk through grief is to walk through something both wild and holy. It does not unfold in straight lines and cannot be explained by logic. And yet, with time and tenderness, we begin to see that each moment of grief is an invitation to excavate the pain and hold it in the light; an opportunity to alchemize our suffering into something sacred.

◎

These pages tell of that journey—of the chaos of mourning, the crushing weight of guilt, and the whispering grace that rises from its depths.

This is the story of how I found joy again—not by turning away from grief, but by walking deeper into it. It's about how history, beauty, and broken buses became part of my healing, how the saints I never expected to care about rose up to meet me, and how a non-religious woman found solace in the sacred—through stone, story, and silence.

This is an offering to all who are walking the same path—those who grieve, who feel guilt, who seek peace, who long to remember joy.

May this book be a companion on your own journey.

PART ONE

The Departure

Leave
behind
the
familiar
world

H1N1

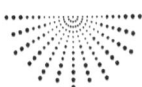

THE SECOND WAVE OF GRIEF

There are hearts ... that never mend again once they are broken.
Or if they do mend, they heal themselves in a crooked and lopsided
way, as if sewn together by a careless craftsman.

— *KATE DICAMILLO*

There are moments in life when we are given the opportunity to recognize that everything is connected; that the path we are wandering intersects in a miraculous way with other paths to form a perfect whole, just as the multicolored threads of a tapestry are woven together to create a magnificent design.

But the design itself is often not visible until much later, when the events of life have further unfolded and we are able to look back and see the patterns that were present all along.

Such an intersection of events occurred for me in the year 2009 and only after several years of contemplation and further unfolding of life's journey have I been able to recognize the presence of miraculous synchronicity during those days of painful exploration.

Life was weaving a tapestry for me then whose beauty I am only now beginning to perceive. The telling of this tale is part of the process of honoring the mystery of life and death and embracing the pain that inevitably accompanies our journeys here on Earth.

T he year 2009 was significant for, among other things, the occurrence of a flu pandemic caused by the H1N1 virus, known as "swine flu." This infectious disease was labeled a public health emergency because of its rapid spread around the world from human-to-human contact. Experts feared a massive death toll from this novel virus and the decision was made to act quickly to lessen the loss of life.

As the medical director of a clinic for low-income and uninsured patients I was briefed as to the potential impact of this pandemic on our community and our clinic in particular, since we served a population of people who generally had limited access to healthcare and preventive medicine.

But 2009 was already marked as an important year for me, months before I heard about the H1N1 flu.

My husband and I were embarking on a new life together as "empty-nesters" after our children left home and we had decided to celebrate this transition with a romantic trip to Italy in September of that year.

We had been doing research for our first-time travel abroad and making plans and reservations for months when I was told that the anticipated date for the deadly H1N1 flu virus to reach our area was "late August or early September," just before our long-planned departure date.

I resolved that I would let nothing get in the way of our trip to Italy, for the survival of my marriage depended on the rejuvenation that would come from that journey—or so I thought.

Determined to take control of this pandemic threat I jumped into action and created an extensive plan for our clinic to make sure we would be able to manage when the flu virus arrived. I ordered the supplies we would need, created training sessions for our staff, and planned for every contingency I could think of.

Yes … I was determined to go to Italy in September knowing that everything was under control in my clinic, pandemic or no pandemic. Nothing was going to interfere with our amazing trip-of-a-lifetime. But I hadn't accounted for the capriciousness of life … and death … and for the reality of impermanence: nothing lasts and everything changes.

That omission would hit me hard and take me down an unexpected path.

F ive days before our departure date for Italy I was attending an all-day retreat for the local hospital board of directors I served on. But I was called into the office because one of our providers had gone home sick leaving a waiting room filled with flu patients and no one to see them.

One of those patients was a 13-year-old boy who had been brought in by his immigrant parents who spoke only Spanish. I can still see his cherubic face as he sat quietly on the exam table listening to my broken medical Spanish and translating his mother's questions.

He was a sweet and gentle boy who was just at the beginning of the illness with a slightly elevated temperature and a mild cough, but he did test positive for the flu. I explained the illness to his parents and advised them that he would likely recover without a problem but they should take him to the emergency room if his symptoms became much worse.

Everything seemed to be going well at the clinic over the next few days and I was confident there would be nothing to worry about there during our 2 weeks of travel. I made one last stop at the clinic on the morning of our departure—to say goodbye, tie up a few loose ends, and reassure myself that all was in order before we left.

B ut the moment I stepped into my office a phone call came: the 13 year-old boy I had seen on Friday, Julio, had been found not breathing by his parents that morning, rushed to the ER by ambulance, and pronounced dead shortly after his arrival.

I could not believe what I was hearing.

There was no possible way, in my mind, that he could have died from the flu. Surely a mistake had been made. I couldn't grasp it and for a moment I simply refused to believe it.

I had planned everything so carefully.

I had created contingencies for every scenario.

I had controlled every variable. This was not possible. This could not happen. But the public health nurse verified the boy's full name and date of birth.

Yes, it was him.

Yes, he was dead.

. . .

An emergency meeting was held to discuss how to make this information public. It was important to "get the messaging right." I sat in stunned silence as I listened to county officials actually talking about "messaging" when a precious boy—my own patient—had just died under my watch.

As the discussion wore on, I was falling apart minute-by-minute and sliding into a deep, dark hole of guilt and grief. I couldn't speak at all and wanted only to run away. Our clinic CEO turned to remind me that I needed to get to the airport for the flight to Italy.

In my shock and numbness I stammered, "I have to cancel the trip."

She was puzzled by the severity of my reaction and waved away my response. "Of course you're not canceling your trip! Just go—I'll take care of everything here."

Just as the CEO couldn't grasp why I was so undone by the news of Julio's death, I too was confused about the depth of despair I was feeling. It took awhile for me to recognize that I had been in this same dark hole of grief and guilt long ago. In fact I had spent years in that murky pit, struggling to keep my head above water, after my father's suicide death.

At that time the grief I experienced was personal—it was devastating to lose my father to suicide. But it was also professional: I was a doctor who had believed that I could prevent bad things from happening to people, especially people I love. I had believed that my knowledge and expertise would allow me to control the circumstances of my life and the lives of those in my presence.

Dad's suicide had shattered that false belief and brought me face-to-face with my own powerlessness over life ... and death. But I had somehow forgotten that lesson and had believed once again that I could control the impact of the H1N1 flu virus and prevent any unfortunate consequence.

When Julio died I was thrown once again into overwhelming grief and guilt as a doctor. I had failed my patient and violated my own vow to save lives.

I remembered with a pang of irony that in medical school I had once written a skit about a doctor who quit medical practice to become a bartender. As I constructed that character and pondered his motivations for leaving medicine I asked myself:

What would make *me* decide to leave this profession I had worked so hard to master?

I had unwittingly written my own story into the history of my character all those years before: he left medicine devastated by the death of a child who was his patient. Now I was living in real life the pain I had created for my fictional doctor/bartender.

I had experienced the deaths of other patients, especially in my work as a hospice physician, but they had all been anticipated and expected deaths. I had not previously felt this massive burden of responsibility and heartache about any other patient death and only later did I recognize that I was reliving the guilt I felt as a doctor over my father's death.

Though I thought I had fully processed all of those emotions during the years I worked in hospice, it was clear that there was still pain and trauma that had been stored away and was now unlocked by Julio's unexpected death.

I didn't know what to call it then, but this trip would become the second wave of my grief—a phenomenon common in complex loss, where sorrow returns months or even decades later, often triggered by anniversaries, transitions, or spiritual awakenings.

As Shelby Forsythia writes:

"The second wave can hit you two weeks after a loss. Or two months. Or two years. Or two decades.

Time is trivial to grief."

What I was feeling was not a gentle return of sorrow. It was sudden, overwhelming, and disorienting. A grief aftershock. As if the volcano I thought long dormant had rumbled to life again—this time asking not just to be remembered, but to be integrated. And it was happening exactly 20 years after my father's death.

Once again I was broken apart by grief and struggling to function. But I had an expensive trip to Italy to navigate and a promise to my husband that this would be a milestone in our relationship as we started a new phase of life. I had no heart for the journey but no way to change what had been planned over the course of the previous year.

So I reluctantly dragged my suitcase—and an overwhelming load of emotional baggage—onto that flight to Rome.

At the time, I couldn't imagine that this unraveling of my life tapestry would become the start of an entirely new design.

But that is the story I'm here to tell.

THE INVITATION

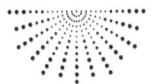

In every moment, the Universe is whispering to you. You're constantly surrounded by signs, coincidences, and synchronicities, all aimed at propelling you in the direction of your destiny.

— DENISE LINN

When we arrived in Rome after 16 hours of travel I was still in a daze. I had not slept at all on the flight and was unable to think about anything except the tragic death of young Julio. But we had a sightseeing itinerary that had been carefully planned for months so I did my best to fulfill those previous expectations. I shuffled through the streets of Rome, going through the motions of looking at ruins and museums without really seeing anything that was in front of me.

Now I not only felt despair over the death of my patient but also over the fact that I was wasting my expensive vacation by not being present enough to take in the experience. But I couldn't shake the negative emotions that were overwhelming me and I couldn't get out from under the pain and guilt I felt inside. I secretly wished that I had canceled the trip and could be dealing with all of this despair from the safety of my own home.

In the afternoon we took off with our guidebook and a small map to try to find our way to the Roman forum. Somehow we got onto the wrong street and couldn't find the entrance we were searching for. We kept walking and walking in the hot sun and became more and more lost as we now could not identify our location on any of the maps we were using.

With frustration rising and our tempers flaring we saw a small church up the road and decided to go inside to escape the heat and figure out where we were. We stepped into the cool, dim interior of the simple little church and sat in a wooden pew at the back. We were alone inside the building but we whispered to one another anyway, not wanting to disturb the peaceful quiet in this calm space.

Finally in our guidebook we found the route we should have followed and saw how to correct our mistake. After a few sips of water we felt refreshed and ready to carry on with our sight-seeing even though I was still in a state of shock and emotional disarray.

My husband stepped outside but I stayed in for a few more moments to look around at the interior of this humble little building, which I later learned was the Church of Saint Bonaventure, a small Franciscan monastery church. It would never have appeared on my list of attractions in Rome. But by some synchronicity we had stumbled across it—a fortunate mistake that would change the course of our entire trip.

I didn't realize that I was looking for something in that space—but I would soon find it.

◎

My overwhelming grief and lack of sleep left me weary and dazed, which added to the surreal and magical feeling inside that church. I walked counterclockwise past a painted crucifix to the right of the altar and small chapels on either side.

As I continued to wander around the pews along the left aisle of the nave, I came across a side chapel where to my surprise a Franciscan friar was seated behind a wooden table. He was wearing the typical brown, hooded robe of a follower of St. Francis, tied with a rope belt at the waist.

On the table in front of him sat a small basket and a sign that read "**Prayer Requests.**" At the time it didn't seem strange to me that the sign was written only in English, but when I saw it I knew somehow that it was meant for me.

I took the pen and one of the small scraps of paper that were resting next to the basket and wrote:

> *"Please pray for the family of Julio Garcia in their grief"*

Then I hastily added,

> *"and for me"*

before folding the piece of paper into fourths and placing it into the basket.

I looked up and the friar was peering directly into my eyes.

Without a word he slowly nodded his head as if to say, "It is already done."

Instantly I felt the weight of grief and guilt lift a bit from my heart for the first time since I learned of Julio's death. I smiled with the relief of being freed momentarily from this burden, whispered "Thank you" to the monk, and turned to walk outside.

As I passed through the door of the little church a word came to my mind that was not familiar to me:

"Novena."

When I looked it up I learned that Novena is a ritual of praying for something desired every day for nine days in a row. I knew instantly that this was a message for me and that I should create my own "grief Novena" during my travels through Italy.

Since our sightseeing itinerary included churches in each city and town we would visit I decided to spend some time every day for the next nine days asking for support for Julio's family and their grief and also for my own intense pain. Creating such a daily ritual would be a way to continue to acknowledge the loss that had occurred and to dedicate a specific time each day to express my sorrow.

I would make space for the grief and welcome it in instead of wishing it would leave me alone. I hoped that I would then be free for the rest of each day to be a tourist in Italy, enjoying the sights and the food without being overwhelmed with so much sadness and guilt.

From that day forward on our trip I continued to carry the memory of Julio's death with me constantly, but the intensity of the grief-aftershock seemed to lift somewhat until the moment I would begin my Novena practice. Then I would be flooded once again with the full deluge of sorrow that poured through me.

Each day I chose a church where we were sightseeing as the location for the Novena prayer and I spent time inside the church walls lighting a candle and whispering my request for help. I contemplated the grief being experienced by Julio's family and my own pain—

as a doctor who lost a patient,

a daughter who lost her father,

a heart-centered physician who wanted to heal others through love,

but who had to accept the reality of life and death.

This mystical moment in the Church of St. Bonaventure— whose name means "good fortune"—was indeed good fortune for me on that day. I later learned that in his childhood Bonaventure was healed of illness by St. Francis himself when the Saint visited his tiny village atop a volcanic mountain, where a swinging bridge—300 feet above a ravine—was the only connection to civilization.

So Bonaventure grew up understanding the value of bridges for bringing together disparate parts. He forged a bridge across the chasm between the mind and the heart with his teachings—that everything comes from the goodness of God and returns to God in a perfect circle of life. This was a visionary concept in Medieval theology—and one that we are still trying to learn and live by now.

Grief can also be a bridge that suspends us precariously above the canyons of loss and longing. It's easy to get stuck there and the crossing can be treacherous.

◎

On that day in Bonaventure's little church, I was lost and couldn't find my way. I needed his unifying wisdom to bridge life and death, grief and joy, the science of medicine and the sacredness of loss. The seen and unseen.

The invitation to enter the depths of my pain came not with words, but through the silent presence of a friar whose simple nod allowed me to feel seen ... witnessed ... held. A doorway opened before me, and I had no idea what lay ahead. But I was willing to take a step—to begin a novena, a pilgrimage of grief, on what was supposed to be a romantic vacation in Italy.

PART TWO

The Descent

Face
adversity
in the
darkness
and find
healing

NOVENA DAY 1

ROME - ST PETERS

Both light and shadow are the dance of Love.

— RUMI

The next morning I woke up exhausted after sleeping only a few hours. I had been tossing and turning, gripped by sorrow and regret, replaying each moment of my visit with Julio and the phone call from the Emergency Room that reported his death. I still couldn't come to terms with the reality of it—a child who was my responsibility had died under my care. It was the fear I had carried since the first day of medical school.

As a mother, I couldn't bear the thought of losing my own child, and my heart ached for Julio's mother in that moment. I was sure she wasn't sleeping either. I knew she was carrying an unspeakable burden of grief, and I was carrying it with her, halfway across the planet.

Eventually, I texted my daughter, knowing it was late afternoon back at home. I finally began to weep as I told her the story, releasing the pain I had been holding in. In the darkness of night, it felt intense and inescapable.

She simply responded, "Oh Mommy, I'm so sorry. Life is just unpredictable, and we really don't have control over it."

She was right. I had been reacting to this tragedy as if I somehow held the power to reverse it—and had failed. But none of what had unfolded was ever in my control. Why then was I so utterly crushed by guilt? How could I ever get out from under its terrible weight? I didn't yet see that the guilt wasn't falling upon me—it was arising from within me, from the depths of my Shadow.

With no answers to my tortured questions, I finally dozed off and slept fitfully until it was time to begin another day of sightseeing.

◉

From our hotel, we wandered the streets of old Rome and marveled at the ruins. I was still in a disoriented haze from sleep loss, the transatlantic flight, and my sudden descent down the grief spiral. My brain was trying to process what had happened and where I was in space and time.

But as we walked across the stones of the ancient Forum and gazed up at soaring columns, massive temples, and crumbling arches, I felt a surprising sense of grounding and familiarity—as if I had been there many times before.

The more time we spent, the stronger that feeling grew. Was it just from seeing photos of Rome in history class? This was more than any déjà vu I'd ever experienced.

I turned to my husband, and at the same time we both said, "I feel like I've lived here before."

. . .

We were encountering the soul of place—that palpable, distinct energy that emanates from locations steeped in deep, layered history. In Rome, from almost any vantage point, you can see the visible strata of her many lives: Roman ruins, Romanesque churches, Medieval streets, Renaissance palaces, Baroque fountains, Neo-classical and Fascist monuments—all tangled together in a chaotic jumble.

But the city pulses with life and soul. You can feel ancestors walking beside you. You can envision the unfolding of humanity over time through the beauty, art, faith, grief, death, and rebirth that rise up from her ancient stones.

From the Forum we moved on to the Colosseum where the atmosphere inside felt heavy and dark. Our guide described the gladiator games once held there and showed us the subterranean tunnels that housed animals and humans before the deadly battles took place in the arena above. This structure was a container for humanity's Shadow, where brutality and violence were glorified and celebrated—and the darkness was palpable.

It's estimated that around 50,000 people were killed in the Colosseum, along with millions of animals sacrificed for sport and entertainment. Stepping inside felt like entering a collective wound—a place that revealed the worst of human potential, where compassion had been forgotten and cruelty took center stage. But it was also a reminder of the full spectrum of human capacity—from glorious to gruesome—a living history book that could hopefully guide us toward our "better angels."

. . .

The Colosseum itself suffered destruction over the centuries, as earthquakes caused the collapse of columns and arches, leaving behind the broken arena we see today. In the Middle Ages, it transitioned into a fortress, a housing complex for families, even a burial ground. Later, it became a quarry—its marble and stones repurposed for new projects, including the construction of St. Peter's Basilica.

Grief born of inhumanity is traumatic and soul-wounding—especially if it is repressed or buried. Humans carry a vast array of trauma wounds to the psyche—ancestral, collective, and personal—and the history of Italy is steeped in them. The underworld can be grotesque, revealing our most abhorrent flaws. But that is only the beginning of the story.

Psychologist James Finley once said, "**Trauma is intermingled with glimpses of the holy.**" Where there is deep pain, there is also the possibility of great transformation—in "the alchemy of love and suffering." What has been buried can become sacred when repurposed. The ruins can become a quarry of raw material for the soul.

This is a truth that unfolds again and again throughout this wild and holy pilgrimage of grief.

@

Our itinerary took us next to the Vatican—the seat of the Catholic Church and a separate city-state within Rome. We were treated to a personalized tour of the Vatican Museum, the Sistine Chapel, and St. Peter's Basilica by my husband's longtime friend, Father William, who served at the time on the Vatican's Council for Interreligious Dialogue.

The thought of a Novena for grief still lingered in the back of my mind, but I had no idea how to "do" a Novena, especially since I'm not Catholic and had long since stepped away from organized religion. My conviction to the idea was wavering as we began our tour of the massive Vatican Museum.

It could take days to see everything there, but thankfully Father William curated a special experience for us. One of the highlights was Laocoön—an ancient Greek statue from 40–20 BCE, rediscovered in 1506 beneath a vineyard.

The sculpture, which depicts a scene from the Trojan War, was recognized by Michelangelo and the Pope's architect as a lost masterpiece once described by Pliny the Elder in his book *Natural History*—a man whose name would surface again later on our journey.

Laocoön's emotional intensity, anatomical detail, and dynamic composition deeply influenced Renaissance artists, including Michelangelo, and helped shape the course of Western art.

This pattern—a lost treasure, buried for centuries, unearthed with world-changing consequences—repeats itself throughout Italy. Vineyards, restaurants, homes, and farms have all serendipitously uncovered ancient ruins just beneath the surface, becoming excavation sites.

But this is also an archetypal truth for each of us.

Deep within lie forgotten treasures—buried memories, ancestral wisdom, inner ruins with power to heal and reshape our future. This is the archaeology of grief. We need only the courage to go inward and begin the excavation....

Later during our tour with Father William I found another piece of art that spoke to me on that particular day. The work was by the Italian artist Caravaggio titled *Deposition from the Cross*. I was awestruck by the powerful images and emotions conveyed in the painting.

Caravaggio depicted the moment just before Christ's body is lowered into the tomb following his crucifixion. John and Nicodemus are bending forward to support the weight of his lifeless body in their arms while the "three Marys"—Virgin Mary, Mary Magdalene, and Mary of Clopas—stand behind. Their faces reflect a symphony of grief: supplication, resignation, silent sorrow, and the shock of final separation. Mary of Clopas reaches upward toward heaven, Mary Magdalene quietly dries her tears, and the Virgin Mary reaches out as if to touch her son in stunned disbelief.

This moment of the physical reality of death is one I was familiar with from hospice work: when the final breath has been expelled and the vital life energy ebbs gradually away from the body, just before it takes on the waxy and unreal appearance of a corpse.

In this painting Jesus still looks as though he could open his eyes and speak; his limbs are still supple, and you can almost feel the warmth still emanating from his skin. Caravaggio has captured this fleeting moment with exquisite skill, and like the mourners in the scene, I found my gaze drawn irresistibly to the form of Jesus, swathed partially in a white sheet.

As I stood mesmerized by the emotional depth of the scene, Father William added another layer of meaning. He pointed out that the drama of this painting is heightened by Caravaggio's use of a technique called *chiaroscuro*, which literally means "light-dark" and relies upon the contrast between dark and light colors to highlight the focal point.

In this painting the body of Jesus and the white shroud that falls away from him attract the eye as they stand out against the black background of the painting and the dark clothing of the mourners. The movement and energy of the painting flows from darkness to light, from life to death, from mourning to hope of resurrection.

I couldn't take my eyes off of the magnificent painting as I contemplated this new word *chiaroscuro*. It was so obvious to me in that moment that the darkness is what makes the light visible.

Without darkness in our lives we would not comprehend the light that exists within us; without death we would not appreciate the life that animates our bodies. The beauty of this life is enhanced because of the darkness, not despite it.

The tragedies of Julio's death and my father's suicide, while unbearably painful, formed a dark background against which I could see, ever more clearly, the vivid luminescence of life. This *chiaroscuro*, the light-dark of existence, is meant to create balance in all things—between joy and sorrow, pleasure and pain, and birth and death.

And I was just beginning to recognize this truth.

As I walked away from the painting, profoundly inspired, I wondered if Caravaggio had intentionally worked to create such a response in the viewers of his creation. Did he himself see the same deeper meaning that had just struck me like a lightning bolt? I can never know the answer to that question, but I did learn more about the story of this Italian artist from the 16th century.

Born Michelangelo Merisi da Caravaggio, he experienced tragedy at age six when most members of his family died of bubonic plague. Orphaned at an early age, he lived on the streets for a time until he became an apprentice to a painter when he was eleven.

Caravaggio probably never recovered from the trauma of those early losses, according to biographers, because he went on to lead a troubled life as an adult. He earned recognition in his lifetime for his prolific paintings, though his subjects and style were sometimes controversial. A taste for alcohol and gambling, along with a violent temper, caused problems throughout his life. At one point he murdered a man and was forced to live as a fugitive during his final years.

Learning this information about Caravaggio's life told me that he was no stranger to tragedy, and that the pain and grittiness visible in his paintings came from real-life experience. He had the ability to portray on canvas the darkness and the light of life here on Earth—all the suffering we must bear as we seek to find meaning in our existence.

There was some solace for me in the intensity of Caravaggio's painting, which seemed to match the intensity of emotion I had been dealing with for the previous few days. I recognized that I was immersed in the swirling waters of life—light and dark, fiery, filled with emotion, and colored by the trauma of being a vulnerable human on a precarious planet.

There was nothing special about the grief I was carrying in that moment—it was the grief that accompanies all of life—but the opportunity existed for me to choose my own unique path through that grief. I could bear it with grace or I could be crushed by it. I could be inspired to live all the more fully by the pain of my grief, or I could give up on life altogether.

In that moment I knew what my choice would be: I would choose life and grace. I would create a beautiful Novena of grief that would contain all of my sorrow and inspire the deepest joy on my journey through Italy. I would willingly go within to explore my own hidden ruins of grief and pain.

Inspired by Caravaggio's painting, I knew I would move forward with the Novena, though I still didn't know what it would look like. When we stopped for a cappuccino break, I asked Father William how it might work for a non-Catholic to perform such a deeply Catholic ritual. He assured me I needn't worry. In his mind, all rituals are available to us for comfort and growth, regardless of our religious practice. He himself had taken up Zen meditation after working in Japan and found it deepened his experience as a Christian.

We moved on toward the Sistine Chapel, eagerly anticipating Michelangelo's much-celebrated paintings on the ceiling and front wall. The room was crowded with tourists as we entered, but there was a noticeable hush throughout the space as each person gazed upward to behold the magnificent ceiling.

The sight was overwhelming at first—too many pictures and scenes to make sense of. But gradually, it came into focus as we listened to an audio guide that led us through Michelangelo's depiction of the story of creation, from the *Separation of Light from Darkness* to the *Drunkenness of Noah* after the great flood.

In the center lies the iconic portrayal of the *Creation of Adam*—with God reaching out with a single finger to delicately transmit the spark of life to Adam's similarly outstretched hand. This image took my breath away: a God who is not overpowering or domineering, but reclining next to Adam, bestowing life to an equal partner—a co-creator of this existence.

The depiction is powerful and gentle at once, as God transmits the awesome force of the entire universe in the slightest touch, as if tending to a fragile being with unconditional loving care. This is the divine breath of life, the moment it enters the physical form—trembling with expectancy, possibility, creativity. The potential for every goodness on Earth lies in this very moment.

I was moved to see these remarkable frescoes, impossibly painted on a barrel-vaulted ceiling—a task that took four years for the reluctant 33-year-old sculptor to complete. Michelangelo never wanted the job and believed he wasn't the best artist to carry it out. But the creation I saw that day told me otherwise.

We sat for a few moments by the marble screen that divides the Chapel, still looking up in wonder at the feat he had accomplished so long ago. Then Father William urged us forward to the wall behind the altar, where another masterpiece awaited.

T*he Last Judgment*, a massive fresco featuring over 300 figures, was painted by Michelangelo 25 years after he completed the ceiling. Inspired by Dante Alighieri's *Divine Comedy*, written 210 years earlier, *The Last Judgment* portrays the moral cosmos that Dante had imagined in his grief-stricken journey through the underworld and back.

Michelangelo's fresco not only reveals the influence of Dante's poem on his thinking—it also shows how similar the two men were in their desire to explore the ultimate questions of life's meaning and what comes after. One used words that painted images in our minds; the other used images that inspired poetic descriptions.

I was beginning to recognize grief as a powerful force that generates creativity and, eventually—perhaps after years of work—transformation.

◎

As we continued our tour through the Vatican, we arrived at last at St. Peter's Basilica. I could not have imagined the immensity of that church, which immediately took my breath away.

This was a stunning contrast to the small and humble church of St. Bonaventure, where I had sat alone the previous day with a silent friar nodding a personal invitation to this pilgrimage. Bonaventure was the church that whispered me onto this inward path. St. Peter's—monumental, majestic, and crowded with pilgrims—would be the church that cracked me open. These two churches formed milestones for my journey—two poles of the sacred: the inner life and the outer life, both essential for growth and transformation.

Inside the awe-inspiring grandeur of St. Peter's, I could easily have gotten lost without the guidance of Father William. He pointed out the enormous stained glass image of golden sunrays surrounding a dove over the altar, the magnificent dome designed by Michelangelo at age 71, the bronze statue of St. Peter whose right toe has been worn smooth by pilgrims touching it as they walk by, and the seven-story bronze canopy designed by Bernini that houses the main altar.

W e ended our walk through the Basilica at a work of art that would become another life-changing source of inspiration: Michelangelo's *Pietà*, a marble statue of Mary holding the lifeless body of her son just after he had been taken down from the cross.

This sculpture depicted the same moment as the Caravaggio painting that had affected me so deeply—the moment just after the last breath, when the life-force is still palpable as it leaves the physical form.

Again I was moved to the core by profound emotion as I beheld Mary, the archetypal Mother of humanity, holding her dead son. In her vast embrace, she was holding all our dead loved ones, helping us carry the sorrow of our humanity.

But Mary was not crushed by her grief. Her expression conveyed peace and acceptance—as if, in her wisdom, she understood that this was a necessary loss, an essential sacrifice that would transform life for the living and therefore must be borne with equanimity.

Of course Mary could help me with my Novena—she understood the pain I was experiencing, and her love was great enough to absorb and transform my grief. In that moment, even as crowds of tourists swarmed against the protective glass in front of the sculpture, I was alone with her.

I felt her strength and courage as she held death in her arms and was not broken by it.

I lit a candle and offered my first Novena prayer:

"Please provide solace to Julio's mother in this moment as she struggles with the greatest pain a mother can bear. And please help me carry the sorrow that fills my heart."

In my mind, I heard the words "Let it be"—lyrics from the Beatles, but a profound message from Mother Mary nonetheless.

"Allow this pain. Let it reside in your heart. Accept this sorrow."

As I connected with her in that moment, I finally understood the power of this Novena ritual I was undertaking. I was only at the beginning, but I was being guided by Mother Mary herself toward the path that would heal and redeem my guilt and grief.

I understood, too, that this Novena was not just for me and my pain. It was a practice on behalf of all: the entire planet, all of creation. As I opened my eyes and lifted my head, I felt a powerful, deep sensation of joy emanate from my heart.

This Novena was going to change everything in my life.

Gazing one last time at Mary and her beloved son, I noticed her left hand—open and turned upward—in a gesture of both hope and release. She has accepted this dreaded cycle of life and death that causes us so much sorrow ... and she has alchemized it with love. This is the glimpse of holiness within the wild terrain of grief.

As we left the Basilica, I stopped at the gift shop to look at the books, artworks, and souvenirs that were available. I wanted a memento, something I could bring with me on this journey to remind me of the peace I felt in Mary's presence. A display of beautiful rosaries caught my eye, particularly one with deep red beads strung together on a silver chain.

The simple circular loop formed by five sets of beads created a roadmap of sorts to an infinite path with no beginning and no end. At its center was a medallion bearing the image of the Madonna and Child—Mary holding baby Jesus in her arms, echoing the *Pietà* that had moved me so deeply. The rosary was a reminder of love holding loss, serenity bearing suffering.

I wasn't Catholic and didn't know the prayers to use with it, but I bought the rosary anyway. It would give me something to hold onto when I felt ungrounded—when I needed to remember that I am not alone in my sorrow. I am resting in the arms of the Divine Feminine.

@

Later I read that Michelangelo was only 24 years old when he sculpted the miraculous *Pietà*, which some have called one of his finest works. He created it from a single block of marble he described as "perfect," and it is the only sculpture he ever signed.

Uniquely, Mary is depicted as much younger than she would have been at the time of Jesus' death—a symbol, it's said, of her incorruptible purity. But it's possible Michelangelo designed his Mary to resemble his own mother, who died when he was just a boy of five or six. Historians say there's no evidence for this idea, but I must disagree.

Of course his artistry was shaped by such profound loss at an early age. Of course his mother's face was etched in his memory, his DNA, every fiber of his being. Of course his grief and longing found expression in his art—whether intentionally or not—

because that is how we humans are made. And that is how grief works.

Grief shapes how we see the world and who we become. It leaves its fingerprints on everything we touch, for all our days.

In this *Pietà*, Mary is not shown in the agony of grief, as many others have depicted her in paintings and sculptures of this exact moment. Her body is strong and stable—capable of holding her grown son and the grief and pain of the entire world—yet her gown is soft and flowing, cascading down to her feet.

Her face, tilted toward her son, is serene and radiant with love. She is still holding her child, still loving him, still mothering him. She has not yet lost the physicality of his presence ... and she somehow knows she will never be separated from his consciousness.

Through close-up photos of this sculpture I later discovered that Mary's gown is draped between the index and middle fingers of Jesus' right hand—in what I see as a precious gesture of a child holding onto his mother for the last time.

Michelangelo seemed profoundly aware of the tender, delicate nature of the love between mother and child, having grieved for his mother all his life. In his *Pietà*, he created a universal mother image for all of us—one that will never die or leave, whose love transcends death and transforms our grief.

No wonder this sculpture has had such a profound effect on people across time and geography—his Mother Mary is a universal icon of grief and enduring love.

©

When people ask me what we did in Italy, my first answer is nearly always: "We walked." Because we did—we walked across cities, from one sacred site to another, through ruins, up staircases, over bridges, along sandy beaches, in olive groves, cathedrals, museums, markets, villages, on grimy streets and flowered alleyways, dirt paths and cobblestones. And it was the best possible therapy for grief. Walking reduced my anxiety and increased tranquility while I processed my emotions. It distracted me from repetitive thoughts and kept me in a state of curiosity because there was always something new and surprising to see.

A favorite ritual we adopted on this trip was the Italian custom of *passeggiata*, which refers to strolling without a particular destination. But for Italians, *passeggiata* is much more than just a casual walk: it's time spent with family and friends, often after work or dinner, that emphasizes socializing and connection more than physical exercise.

Stepping out onto the sidewalk near our hotel that evening in Rome, we were immediately swept into a gentle flow of people—walking slowly, talking, laughing, sometimes shouting *ciao!* to someone across the street, and stopping often to emphasize a story or admire a garden or store window.

The essence of the *passeggiata* seemed to be joy—an exuberant embrace of life and people and memory and health and connectedness and simply being here in this moment, in this place. I had never experienced anything like it and couldn't wait to join the locals in this ritual wherever we stayed.

This passion for life and all it entails—including grief and loss—is so deeply ingrained in Italian culture that it forms the foundation for the soul of place, which is tangible in every city and village. While walking in the flow of *la dolce vita*—the sweet life—I found it much easier to carry my grief and also allow joy to have a presence.

That night we strolled from Piazza del Popolo to the Spanish Steps, taking it all in—exhausted from a full day of sightseeing and emotion, but alive with the energy of this place and ready to engage it.

We saw a sweet little outdoor café down a narrow side street and stopped for dinner, ordering something familiar to help us keep our bearings in these new surroundings: caprese salad and ravioli, with bread, olive oil, and red wine. We tore pieces of bread and dipped them gently into the greenish-gold oil, in between sips of the fruity wine.

This was a communion of sorts, a toast to our accomplishment of finally arriving in Italy—grief wounds and all—and beginning to savor every moment.

It was enough. Tomorrow, I would begin again, uncertain about what might happen next, but filled with the quiet presence of something wild and holy.

Held

Today I recognize
I am not really alone
in my grief
even though
it feels like it at times.
The pain I have experienced
is part of the suffering
of the Universe
and not unique to me.
But I am held **always**
in the broken heart
of the Divine Feminine.
I believe this grief
is a portal
a doorway
to something greater.
To transformation.
And I am ready for it.

NOVENA DAY 2

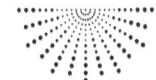

ROME - TRASTEVERE

Grief and love are sisters, woven together from the beginning. Their kinship reminds us that there is no love that does not contain loss and no loss that is not a reminder of the love we carry for what we once held close.

— FRANCIS WELLER

The following morning I awoke to see my red rosary on the nightstand, coiled into an infinity symbol. I reached out to touch it and remembered that I am being held ... always ... in unseen arms of Divine love.

Much later I would hear an interview with poet David Whyte where he said that you will know you are on your path when you can't see the path before you. So there I was in Rome with an itinerary that no longer made sense, on a grief journey I hadn't planned, and without knowing what to expect next.

Something profoundly spiritual was happening for me even though I didn't recognize it at the time.

After breakfast at our hotel we walked to Capitoline Hill to see the statue of Marcus Aurelius and tour the adjacent museum. Marcus Aurelius was known as the last of "Five Good Emperors" of Rome. He ruled during the end of the Pax Romana (Roman Peace) and was a Stoic philosopher, still revered today for his writings. His Meditations, which he is believed to have written as a private diary to himself, are filled with the wisdom of one who strove to be the best person he could be during a life filled with challenges and loss.

His statue depicts a man of power, yet peace—his right hand extended in what appeared to be a gesture of mercy or grace. But his face, to me, revealed a sadness at the heavy burdens of life.

In fact a deadly plague lasting fifteen years spread throughout the Roman Empire in 165 AD when he was emperor, causing 2,000 deaths per day in Rome with total lives lost estimated at 5 million. Plagues and pandemics have been ravaging human society for centuries and throughout history people have mourned the pain of each unexpected death. What I was experiencing was nothing new—the pain of being in a position of responsibility over something that cannot be controlled or contained.

After losing three of his children Marcus wrote, "One man prays: 'How I may not lose my little child', but you must pray: 'How I may not be afraid to lose him.'"

This wisdom resonates with me. As a wife, mother, doctor, caregiver, friend, neighbor I must learn to live with the reality of death and the quiet anxiety it brings. It is necessary to carry this fear amidst all the joys and goodness of life and not be daunted or paralyzed by it. I can imagine that throughout history there have been shamans and healers and curanderos and midwives and physicians who have carried grief and guilt over the lost lives of children.

But on the day I received the call from the emergency room, *I* was the doctor who had been pulled out to sea by the wild riptide of grief and I wondered whether or not I could withstand the force. Would I be dashed and washed up on some rocky shore? I didn't yet know the answer.

We had tickets that morning to tour the Borghese Gallery, one of the most famous art galleries in the world, which had been highly recommended. The villa was formerly a cardinal's mansion built in the early 17th century and the building itself is a work of art, surrounded by beautiful gardens. The lavishly decorated rooms house masterpieces including Roman statues, Baroque paintings, and works by renowned artists such as Caravaggio, Raphael, Titian, and Bernini.

I was in awe from the moment I entered the villa to see the interior decor with carved marble facades, intricately painted ceilings, and impressive artwork in every room.

But the most stunning moment occurred when I stepped inside the third room on the first floor to see a life-size marble sculpture by Gian Lorenzo Bernini depicting the mythical story of *Apollo and Daphne*. It captures the precise moment when Daphne, running from Apollo's lovesick grasp, is metamorphosing into a laurel tree. Apollo's hand touches her just at the moment her body begins to transform with her feet shaped as roots into the earth, her fingers becoming leaves, her skin turning into tree bark as she begins to dissolve away.

There is a look of both desire and agony on Apollo's face as he realizes that he cannot hold onto his beloved. And Daphne expresses a mixture of fear and surrender, recognizing that she cannot change her fate.

Bernini's skill at portraying movement and emotional intensity made it feel as if we had just stumbled across this pair at the exact moment of crisis, the last breath, the slipping away that cannot be prevented. Apollo is every human being trying to hold onto the life of a loved one during that heartbreaking moment when life transforms before their eyes. His grief is palpable with the realization that he cannot stop what is happening ... it is out of his control.

This is a moment I have seen before: in emergency rooms, in hospice beds, in the eyes of a mother clinging to her child, in my own heart and hands struggling to reverse what is inevitable. This is what grief looks like exactly at the moment of loss.

It is wild, surging, grasping, desperate.

And it is holy—as the reaching hand fills only with the star-dust of a form dissolving away in sacred surrender.

We live these transient lives to the best of our ability when we cannot see the larger picture that is unfolding—the arc of the entire Universe, the narrative of human existence, and the meaning of each and every moment that is given to us. So of course we grasp for more—more time, more love, more success, more control. We always believe we can hold onto what we love ... that *this* time somehow we'll find a way. But then life transforms before our eyes and under our touch and we are helpless to change it.

Over and over again as a doctor I have been humbled to remember my ultimate powerlessness.

Some people get better ...

some people stay the same ...

and all people eventually die.

This is a tough reality for medical providers. What motivates us if we cannot actually change the outcome? Perhaps we are looking at the wrong outcome. We are chasing after life thinking we can preserve it unchanged ... but everything changes.

Can we witness life as it transforms and bring our love and compassion into the moment without fear? Can we hold the hand that is dissolving away?

@

On our tour I found out that Gian Lorenzo Bernini, a prodigy of art since childhood, had been commissioned to create the Apollo and Daphne sculpture along with three others that are housed in the Borghese Gallery. His particular skill was in portraying intense emotion and psychological drama at the moment of crisis—so the viewer is immediately caught up in the scene and awash with the same emotion.

His many sculptures that can be viewed throughout Rome are all masterpieces of physical and emotional realism—even some massive works like the Four Rivers Fountain and the canopy over the tomb of St. Peter. What intrigued me about Bernini was his apparent emotional intelligence, which seemed rare for a man in the 16th century.

Unlike Michelangelo there is no historical evidence that Bernini suffered great trauma in his early life that catalyzed his creative genius—he seems to have been born with sensitivity to the human condition.

But later in life he joined a Jesuit Confraternity of the Bona Mars to study the "art of dying happily" and he spent the rest of his life keeping death always present in his thoughts. Indeed his son wrote that the artist's death was peaceful and devotional—another masterpiece he left as part of his legacy. That image of a death approached with devotion, as a final creation rather than a failure, resonated with me.

I was experiencing once again that I was not alone in grief or in death. These are the thoughts that arose for me at every stop throughout this journey. Viewing Italy through a lens of grief helped me move more slowly and mindfully amongst her many treasures. No matter what I encountered I saw both life and death unfolding everywhere—and it was breathtaking.

Contemplating the darkness helped me see the light so clearly —*chiaroscuro*—and that pattern was already emerging as a theme for this pilgrimage through Italy.

The site of the Apollo and Daphne statue had transported me into a liminal space of grief where grasping was giving way to surrender—to the quiet acceptance that some things cannot be changed. We simply do not have control. I continued to think of that breathtaking sculpture as we left behind the Borghese Gallery and walked back in time from the Renaissance to the era of Ancient Rome.

I found myself still thinking about our human desire to control life and death—the desire to touch the eternal even as our bodies betray us—as we came upon one of Rome's greatest mysteries: the Pantheon. Built in the second century CE the Pantheon has somehow stood untouched and majestic through centuries—its perfect symmetry and impossible engineering reaching up toward the heavens. Humans may not be able to find immortality within our own physical bodies, but we have managed to build some structures that border on the eternal.

It's hard to find words to describe the feeling you get when you step through the massive bronze doors of the Pantheon, but the space inside is so vast and harmonious that if feels almost cosmic — a circle of the Universe shaped by perfection itself. Even your own heartbeat seems to slow down in the presence of such sacred awe. The marble floor is constructed with a complex pattern of squares and circles, in shades of deep red, golden yellow, and creamy white. There is a slow-moving beam of light coming from above that gives the entire structure a gentle glow. The walls are covered in rich marbles from across the ancient world — purple, green, and golden — with impressive Corinthian columns.

But the most spectacular feature is the dome, a perfect hemisphere made of square coffers that diminish in size near the top as they form a great open oculus at the center—the eye of heaven, some people call it. It is impossible not to look up, as the geometry of the dome draws the eye upward to contemplate heaven. There are myths that say it serves as a gateway or portal to the divine, always open, always connecting the gods to us in our human challenges.

Through the oculus pure light streams down, casting a perfect circle on the marble floor below. The light moves slowly across the interior, silently marking time. The entire structure is both deeply human — built by hands like mine — and utterly divine, beyond the reach of our full understanding, wild and holy at once.

The knowledge of how the Pantheon was constructed was lost for centuries after Rome's fall, forgotten during darker times in the natural cycle of life. Though humans lost the wisdom needed to reach for the heavens, the Pantheon continued to stand— oblivious to human struggles. The light continues to reach down through the oculus to illuminate the shadows so we can see our way in the darkness.

I would later read that one secret to the long survival of the Pantheon has been discovered: its ancient concrete contains tiny lime clasts—fragments that allow it to self-heal over time when water seeps in. The structure mends itself through the very substance of its making, as though even stone can learn to restore what has been broken.

Perhaps our hearts are built the same way.

Though the immense dome was filled with tourists that day, I stood there in a hush, watching the play of light and shadow, *chiaroscuro*. I thought: this, too, represents grief and hope woven together — sorrow contained in every stone, but hope that lies within the persistence of the shelter itself, that survived when memory and empire had failed, that found a way to heal when it seemed impossible.

Eventually, we stepped back into the streets of Rome, leaving behind the ancient to see what might be discovered by wandering in the present moment.. The memory of the Pantheon's moving circle of light stayed with me as I walked across the city, through narrow winding alleys and sunlit piazzas, across the Tiber River on an old stone bridge, the Ponte Sesto, to the quaint working-class neighborhood of Trastevere. Compared to the busy city atmosphere of Rome, Trastevere felt like a medieval village with cobblestone streets that wound through family-run shops and restaurants.

We had come to visit the Basilica of Santa Maria in Trastevere, which fronted a large piazza at the heart of the district. Children were playing soccer on the square while their parents watched from the steps of the beautiful central fountain.

Father William had guided us there because Santa Maria is one of the oldest churches in Rome, founded in the 3rd century CE and dedicated, of course, to Mother Mary. He wanted us to see the stunning gold mosaic from the 12th century that decorates the apse behind the altar. I thought Santa Maria might be a good location for my second Novena prayer but I didn't yet realize how perfectly circumstances had aligned.

We entered the dimly lit interior of the church and as our eyes adjusted we could see a group of people crowded into the pews in front of the altar. We quietly took a seat in the back row, not wanting to disturb them. As we studied the spectacular golden domed mosaic glittering and looming above the altar, we gradually realized we were witnessing a funeral—for there, among the mourners, stood a casket.

How was it possible that we had walked into that church during a funeral?

How had the timing been that precise when we had no particular schedule or plan?

Of course. This was the perfect next stop on my wild journey of grief. My heart cracked open once again as I was transported back to our home town where I imagined that Julio's funeral might be taking place as this very moment, as well.

I sat in silence and took in the words of the priest, though of course I didn't understand the language. But I perceived the meaning of what was being spoken and I resonated with the grief that poured from the hearts and voices of the mourners. I was being provided with an opportunity to experience what I had missed out on at home—the chance to mourn in community with others who knew the weight of loss.

With soft tears I recalled Julio's sweet face when he spoke with me that day in the clinic; and I also remembered every syllable from the final conversation I had with my father. Those words are engraved in my memory—words I didn't know would be the last—words that now carry all the weight of my grief.

I said the second Novena prayer through tears as I witnessed a stranger's funeral.

"Please bring healing and wellbeing to Julio's family and friends and may they forgive me if I have done anything to cause them harm."

I also asked my father to forgive me—

for not saving him,

for not creating a miracle,

for not being capable of redirecting the course of the Universe,

for being a healer that can't always heal,

for being a student of love in a classroom where pain is the curriculum.

And—though I didn't see it for a very long time—I was really asking for help to forgive *myself* for all of those things I could not do, for all of my failures, and all of my humanness.

As I poured out my grief and doubt and guilt inside that church during a funeral for a stranger I felt, once again, the presence of the Divine Mother, gazing down with serene compassion and gesturing so simply: *It's okay. Let it be.*

Even a stranger's grief can help you find your own.

A s we walked quietly through the church before leaving I dropped my guidebook and when I reached down to pick it up I noticed that the marble flooring consisted of a stunning array of intricate geometric patterns. There were small circles, squares, diamonds, stars, and triangles of stone and glass inlaid into interlocking infinity symbols that snaked up the central aisle of the church. The design was beautiful and mesmerizing in its flow, a powerful expression of sacred geometry.

Later I viewed even more magnificent floors in the Church of Santa Maria Maggiore and learned that they and several others throughout Rome were created by a four-generation family of master artisans—the Cosmati--in the 12th and 13th centuries. The patterns are filled with symbolism and designed to lead visitors toward the altar.

Some mystery surrounds these sacred geometric layouts as the Cosmati kept their techniques and hidden symbolic meanings shrouded in secrecy. But they are seen as maps of the universe, reflecting divine order and the structure of the cosmos.

Galileo would later say that the universe is written in the language of mathematics — triangles, circles, and geometric figures. These floors spoke that language in stone and reminded me that there is order in the universe ... even when it feels as if the Earth I trod is spinning off its axis. And there are mysteries too deep and vast to comprehend.

Following the somber synchronicity of the funeral at Santa Maria in Trastevere we walked in silence for awhile. Already the emotions for this day had been intense and though I was still feeling a bit dazed and in-between worlds I was beginning to recognize that grief is everywhere. While I had initially felt isolated and alone with my broken heart it was clear that I was being guided somehow to witness the grief of others as an essential aspect of being human.

Even the floors of the church had spoken to me that there is something grander in creation than the story I live within.

With my rosary in my pocket I sensed a glimmer of connection to the grieving family in the church, to the mythical figures of Apollo and Daphne, to an ancient emperor of Rome, and an orphaned Renaissance artist. Something was beginning to awaken within the wreckage of my heart.

We strolled along the banks of the Tiber River until we spotted a tiny island in the middle of the river and decided to cross over to check it out. There we found an old hospital, still operational, that had secretly housed people who fled the Jewish quarter during World War II when Nazis were rounding up Jews to send to concentration camps.

Remarkably the doctors and nurses on staff had hidden dozens of people in a ward at the back of the hospital and protected them by inventing a fictitious "fatal infectious disease" that required strict isolation. Those "patients" were never caught and somehow every staff member of that hospital had managed to keep their hiding place secret.

This extraordinary act of courage—resilience and creativity in the face of evil—touched my heart and reminded me that pain is all around us ... but so too is hope. We can find our way to grace when we look out for one another and honor the sacredness of our connections with everyone, regardless of their identity.

We are all one people ... one life ... one grief.

B efore we continued the next steps of our journey I bought a bouquet of sunflowers from a vendor at the hospital. The path took us across one more bridge over the river, the Ponte Fabricio, which was built in the year 62 BCE.

How had this structure stood unharmed for over 2000 years?

I stopped to imagine all the feet that had walked this crossing throughout those years—merchants transporting their wares to Rome, centurions marching off to battle, pilgrims trekking to a holy site, Jews fleeing the Nazi invasion, workers returning home after a day of toil, parents rushing a sick child to the hospital.

So much life has passed over the worn stones of this ancient bridge ... and in that moment the trajectory of my own life intersected with that very passageway. A portal between what had been and what was to be; a liminal space where I was no longer the same person I had been the day before.

I dropped each sunflower into the water to honor all who had entered this portal in grief, in fear, in love, in celebration, in pain, in loss.

I released my attachments to the life I thought I was living.

I let go of who I thought I was.

I surrendered my control over how life and death should unfold.

As I watched each flower float away gently on the slow current my tears mingled with the river, sanctifying all the interrupted and imperfect lives that have always been connected to my own.

There is no separation ... I could see that for the first time.

We exited the Ponte Fabricio and entered Rome's Jewish Quarter—one of the most ancient Jewish communities in the world. Our plan was simply to pass through on the way back to our hotel after an eventful day. But as we reached the plaza ahead, it was clear something special was happening.

There was music, laughter, warm conversation, and people coming together. Dressed in their finest, they gathered around tables and under canopies, sipping glasses of wine and passing baskets of bread and apples.

A waiter told us it was Rosh Hashanah—the start of the Jewish New Year.

Caught up in the joyous celebration and feeling our own hunger and weariness, we asked for a table at the nearby café.

A New Year—what a perfect celebration to mark this point on my grief pilgrimage. In Rome I had experienced a loss, received a sacred call to Novena, encountered the embrace of Divine Love, and shared in rituals of mourning and release.

What a fitting day to end up in the right place at the right time— to honor the beginning of something new.

We asked the waiter to bring us whatever was on the menu for Rosh Hashanah. And in view of the holiday joy unfolding around us, we feasted on chicken and honeyed fruit, crispy artichokes, couscous, and dates. We dipped apple slices into honey and I tasted the sweetness of life emerging—wild and also holy.

Grief and joy can sit side by side at the same table. And together, we can all partake in this bittersweet feast that is life.

Woven

I have carried this grief
for so long
it is woven through
my blood and bones
and shapes my footprints
in the sand.
Though I neglected it for years
it runs to greet me
when the door opens
like a child whose parent returns at last.
I am here now.
I will take you in my arms
and not let go.
You are mine.
You are LOVE.

NOVENA DAY 3

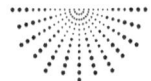

FLORENCE - SANTA MARIA DEL FIORE

There is a vastness to grief that overwhelms our minuscule selves. We are tiny, trembling clusters of atoms subsumed within grief's awesome presence. It occupies the core of our being and extends through our fingers to the limits of the universe.

— NICK CAVE

The moment I stepped into the city of Florence, I was in awe of the beauty and history that permeate every stone and structure. The soft colors, the narrow winding streets, the play of light and shadow—it was like stepping into a painting remembered from a dream. There is a tangible sense of aliveness here—growth and creativity born not only from human ingenuity but from centuries of sorrow.

That energy seems to spring from the tragic history of the plague and the astonishing resurgence of beauty and hope that followed. It truly feels like a miracle to behold a city that is both a mausoleum of the Black Death and the cradle of the Renaissance, where grief gave birth to brilliance.

I n 1348, Florence lost nearly 60% of its population to the plague. Imagine losing more than half of all the people you know and live alongside in your community. The loss was staggering, both individually and collectively. The city struggled with labor shortages, a collapse of services, and tens of thousands of unclaimed bodies that had to be buried in mass graves. Funeral rites were abandoned out of fear. Families had no time to grieve one death before another occurred, unraveling the fabric of their lives.

Day-to-day life literally ground to a halt. Art stopped. Commerce ceased. Everything paused as survivors reeled from the overwhelming loss of all they had known. The city was devastated physically and emotionally—shattered by a grief too immense to express or even bear. Faith itself faltered, shaken by prayers that went unanswered in the face of unimaginable suffering.

But the Black Death is not what makes Florence unique. All of Europe was ravaged by the plague. Florence is remarkable for what came after. In the century that followed, the city conceived, midwifed, and nurtured the Renaissance—the miraculous rebirth of culture, art, science, architecture, philosophy, religion, and exploration. And not just a rebuilding of what had been lost, but a transcendence—a leap to a new stage of consciousness that reshaped the world.

Historians have identified many contributing factors: a reshuffling of the population and the cross-pollination of ideas as people moved in search of safety or work; the redistribution of wealth that gave rise to new patronage; the blossoming of scientific inquiry sparked by a desire to understand the body and disease. Artists turned to themes of death and human frailty. Thinkers asked deeper questions about life and meaning. And all of it unfolded not despite the grief, but through it.

The Renaissance was a response to the deepest possible sorrow —a collective cracking open that did not deny the pain but revealed the brilliance hidden within it. The plague broke the world apart, and light poured in through the fissures. *Chiaroscuro*—light and darkness, wild and holy, grief and transcendence. This is the palpable tension that vibrates throughout Florence.

And on this pilgrimage of grief, I was being cracked open too —so I could finally glimpse that same transcendent view of life and death.

@

One cannot visit Florence without being drawn to the vast array of art housed within the city, and Michelangelo's statue of David is perhaps the most iconic of all—attracting visitors from around the world. The statue resides in the Accademia Gallery and is breathtaking in both scale and craftsmanship. Michelangelo was a master of expressing emotion, even in unyielding stone, as we had already seen in Mary's serene, sorrowful gaze in the *Pietà*.

Just as Bernini captured the single, liminal moment before Daphne's transformation, Michelangelo portrayed David in the precise instant before he hurls a stone at Goliath. The look on David's face reveals his awareness of the moment's gravity. He radiates fearlessness and resolve, but there's also a trace of sorrow in his eyes.

This is the sacred pause before everything changes—and we, too, are suspended in that pause with him.

Michelangelo was no stranger to grief. As we've already seen, he lost his mother at the age of six. He lived much of his adult life in sadness and solitude, and he etched his suffering into stone and fresco—into walls and ceilings and silent marble figures. Burdened by his work, haunted by spiritual anguish, and often embroiled in conflict, Michelangelo expressed his grief not in words, but in form.

The Renaissance arose from the ashes of the Black Death, and death left its mark on the artists who emerged from that crucible. Michelangelo wrestled with mortality and the human condition, and from that struggle he drew magnificence. His David was carved from a single piece of marble—discarded by other sculptors as too damaged, too narrow, too flawed to be of any use. Much like Michelangelo's own life, the block was deemed unsuitable.

But he saw something inside. He found the courageous figure hidden in the stone, and—as he famously said—he "just removed everything that is not David."

He took what had been cast aside and made it a masterpiece. That is the invitation grief offers each of us.

Can we carry the stone of loss and find beauty within it? Can we slowly chip away all that is not love?

Michelangelo lived his sorrow—but he transformed it through his art, and in doing so, he helped transform the world.

This message from Florence became unmistakably clear:

Devastation can be the doorway to transformation.

Don't turn away.

Let grief sculpt you into someone new.

Leaving the Accademia, still steeped in the presence of sculpture, Florentine art, and musical instruments, we stepped outside to wander the streets of Florence—the very streets Michelangelo once walked—worn smooth with time, unchanged for centuries. The terracotta walls leaned close in some of the narrow corridors, accented with flowerboxes overflowing from windows above, trailing geraniums and verbena.

The soul of place vibrates through all of Florence with a creative spark that rises from profound and meaningful sorrow. Everywhere, there are signs of rebirth: frescoes that outlived fire, sculptures that survived siege, beauty that bloomed after plague. Somehow, I felt fully alive in a city that has known so much death.

But the past and present merge constantly in busy Florence. You can wander down a hushed Medieval alley, turn a corner, and suddenly find yourself thrust into a modern swirl of scooters, honking horns, weaving bicycles, delivery vans, and pedestrians in leather jackets and high heels navigating the cobbled streets.

There is a joyous and dizzying flow to Florence that sweeps you along, compelling you to keep walking, to keep exploring—for there is always something unexpected waiting to be discovered.

As we wandered through a patchwork of streets, still awestruck from viewing the magnificent David, the sky suddenly broke open in a downpour. Seeking shelter, we dashed into the nearest doorway—and were instantly transported into another world.

We had stumbled into the Officina Profumo-Farmaceutica di Santa Maria Novella, the world's oldest pharmacy, founded in 1221 by Dominican friars from the Santa Maria Novella convent. The friars had once cultivated medicinal herbs to create remedies, balms, and pomades for the monastery's infirmary. Remarkably, the shop has been in continuous operation ever since, and still sells perfumes, soaps, and lotions made from the original recipes—using herbs and natural ingredients grown in Tuscany.

In the Old Apothecary Room where we entered, tall cabinets of polished wood held glass jars filled with fragrant herbs and bottles of elixirs, potions, and salves. The air was heavy with an earthy, soulful blend of lavender, thyme, rosemary, cloves, and citrus. We marveled at a display featuring an elegant perfume first created for the wedding of Catherine de Medici in 1533— still unchanged across the centuries. It felt as though time had folded in on itself in that magical place.

When I stepped up to the counter to purchase a bottle of Catherine's Acqua della Regina, the shopkeeper noticed we were soaked and shivering. With great kindness, she invited us to their tea room to warm ourselves until the storm passed.

We were seated at a small round table by a window overlooking a courtyard filled with apple trees. The room was quiet, the world hushed by rain drumming on the roof and streaming down the glass. A server brought us Melissa tea—blended with star anise, linden flowers, lemon balm, fennel, peppermint, and chamomile—along with tiny shortbread cookies and jasmine chocolates.

This unexpected interruption in our day felt like a welcome relief after the intensity of museum-going. It was a moment of deep rest and solitude in a space that echoed with old-world grace. I imagined the artists and philosophers, monks and seekers, who might have once sought refuge here from the storms of life—healing their wounds with tinctures and teas, and with silence.

I, too, was being healed.

Grief had sculpted this journey from the beginning and continued to chip away at what was no longer needed—revealing, little by little, the wild and the holy that had always been hidden within.

We returned to our wandering after the rain retreated and found the entire city aglow with shimmering light. The ancient stones—freshly washed—reflected golden beams of sunlight peeking through the clouds.

Another moment of transcendent beauty in this surreal city, shaped by both rain and sun, grief and grace.

We stopped by the Galileo Science Museum, where we learned about two of Florence's brilliant sons who lived in different centuries and who both had a lasting influence on Western culture: Dante Alighieri and Galileo Galilei.

Dante, primarily known as a 14th century poet, was also a physician, mathematician, geologist, and cosmographer, as we learned from an exhibit in the museum. He wrote his epic poem *The Divine Comedy* over a span of 15 years while exiled from Florence for his political views.

Dante grieved both the loss of his beloved city and the death a woman he admired from afar: Beatrice. He made her a central character in *The Divine Comedy* where she ultimately guides him from the fires of purgatory toward God. Described as one of the most impressive poems ever created—with more than 14,000 lines—the work portrays a true Hero's Journey of transformation as it maps the moral landscape and ultimately leads the reader to Divine Love.

As we already discovered, Michelangelo's fresco of the Last Judgment on the wall of the Sistine Chapel was inspired by Dante's depiction of Hell. Then we learned in this museum that Galileo had lectured on *The Divine Comedy* during the early years of his career—some 270 years after it was written.

Dante's influence has echoed through centuries of poets, authors, artists, and theologians. One professor of literature wrote that he read Dante daily for years while grieving his wife's death in childbirth, finding solace in the poet's words about the "love that moved the sun and the other stars."

The poetry of grief resonates across centuries and continents.

F lorence's other son, the namesake of the gallery, was one of the most revolutionary minds in history. Galileo Galilei, a Renaissance visionary, was famously condemned as a heretic by the Catholic Church for supporting Copernicus' radical theory: that the sun, not the Earth, stood at the center of the solar system. But there is so much more to Galileo than that single, tragic headline.

He built telescopes capable of observing the stars of the Milky Way, the surface of the moon, and distant planets. He made groundbreaking contributions to astronomy, motion, mathematics, engineering, physics, and even sound. He was also a gifted artist—always sketching, drawing, or painting what he saw in the heavens or uncovered in his experiments. Early in life, he taught at a school of art and design, captivated by the use of perspective and *chiaroscuro*—light and shadow.

Galileo was a brilliant thinker who saw what others could not—and suffered the consequences. Sentenced to house arrest for the final decade of his life, he was forbidden from teaching or speaking of his "heretical" ideas, which he was forced to recant publicly. For a scientist devoted to truth, it must have been excruciating to be silenced by those who hadn't yet caught up to his insight.

As if the loss of his freedom wasn't enough, just four months into his confinement, Galileo's beloved daughter died of an acute infection. She had been a Poor Clare nun, cloistered in a convent, and had taken the spiritual name Celeste—honoring her father's devotion to the heavens. Her death devastated him. She had been his confidante, his emotional and spiritual support during the agonizing years of the Inquisition. Still, he carried on, turning to writing as a refuge from grief. His final book, *Two New Sciences*, was completed in that painful solitude.

I n that moment, while contemplating Galileo's tragic life—I glimpsed a memory of a much-younger me who chose to "recant" my own mystical inner knowing that felt too fragile and mysterious to share with the world. I had gathered all the poems I had written from that place of knowing and burned them to protect their truth.

I had exiled my most precious self—caging the wild to protect its holiness. And this place is where my exiled grief had lived for years as well, waiting to be reclaimed.

No one is exempt from grief—not the most brilliant thinker, the most gifted artist, the most expressive poet, the kindest soul, or the most devoted father. Galileo's life revealed the transformative power of adversity and sorrow to shape one's creativity, purpose, and legacy.

G alileo once wrote:

"I've loved the stars too fondly to be fearful of the night."

The stars Galileo observed through his telescope are the same stars I gaze upon each night—the same ones that have fascinated humankind for millennia. Every culture has created myths and cosmologies around the night sky, often interpreting its lights as echoes of death, longing, and loss.

The Milky Way itself has long been seen as a celestial pathway for the souls of the dead—a parallel to the oculus of the Pantheon dome, a round eye opening to eternity.

No doubt, countless mourners have looked up at those stars and searched for the presence of a beloved one now gone.

Galileo mapped the Pleiades constellation, known in mythology as the Seven Sisters—who, according to legend, died of grief and were placed in the heavens by Zeus to shine forever. With his telescope, Galileo identified over 40 stars in that cluster. Today, we know there are thousands. He revealed that the Milky Way was not a painted ribbon of light, as once thought, but a "mass of innumerable stars."

T hese myths are not arbitrary or quaint. We are wired to be enchanted by the stars and comforted by their steadfast glow in the dark sky. And now science tells us why: we are made of stardust. The same elements forged in supernovas form our bones, our breath, our blood.

The mysteries of the stars echo the mysteries of our own human form. They give shape to the unknown and are vast enough to contain our grief—grief that sometimes spills beyond the limits of our own emotional gravity.

On this journey through Italy, I was being shown not just an archaeology of grief but a cosmology as well—a longing that shines eternal in the night sky, balancing the descent into the inner darkness of sorrow. One draws us inward, deeper into our own pain. The other lifts our gaze to the infinite. And we walk between them—on this wild and holy path of grief.

Walking on through narrow streets that twisted and turned while tall buildings obscured our view, we began to wonder if we'd lost our way. Then, suddenly, we turned a corner and there it was: Santa Maria del Fiore Cathedral, towering above the square in the heart of Florence's historic center.

This stunning church, layered with marble in shades of green and pink, took over 140 years to build—its construction delayed for decades during the plague. And yet the city eventually rebounded to complete this extraordinary Duomo, a lasting testament to resilience and hope after devastation.

The completion of the dome—a monument to both ingenuity and hope—was an architectural miracle. It was built entirely without scaffolding, something never before attempted. Renaissance architect Filippo Brunelleschi, inspired by the Pantheon in Rome, designed the improbable octagonal dome and invented several custom machines to achieve this feat of engineering. It was yet another example of how the devastation of the plague eventually gave rise to breathtaking transcendence, a century later.

To step inside the Duomo is to feel instantly small as the vast, cool, shadowed space rises above you. Even though tourists fill the aisles and form long lines before each chapel, there is a sacred hush that quiets the mind and grounds the soul. Compared to the ornate splendor of St. Peter's, this cathedral is modest—but the soul of place here is deep, inviting you to go within.

And then you look up.

The miraculous dome, with its eight ribs, draws your vision toward the center where Giorgio Vasari's breathtaking fresco of the Last Judgment spreads across the ceiling. Light streams through high windows, illuminating different portions of the painting depending on the time of day.

I stood in stillness, softened and humbled by all I had seen that day—from the horrors of the Black Death to the transcendence of the Renaissance; from Michelangelo's sorrow that birthed his art, to the healing medicine of old ways, to the stars that contain our grief. I was still carrying my own pain—resurfaced, raw at times—but I stood in a city that had been reborn again and again across the centuries.

The ache of being human was palpable, woven into the architecture, layered into the stones. But I could also feel the vastness of collective resilience—the creativity that arises from suffering. In that improbable church, under that miraculous dome, I carried it all: sorrow and splendor, loss and legacy.

I walked to the space dedicated to the Virgin Mary and lit a votive candle. Taking a long, slow deep breath, I could feel the loving arms of the Divine Feminine as I whispered my quiet Novena prayer:

"May my pain lessen the pain of Julio's family, and of all who grieve in this moment. May our connectedness bring comfort to us all and inspire creativity for healing."

These simple prayers, along with the stillness and presence I felt inside the churches, were changing me. There was still pain—and more grief rising to the surface each day—but there was also Love, enfolding and illuminating me. I was ready to continue on this Novena path.

Much later I would come across an article that reminded me of this experience—gazing up at Brunelleschi's magnificent dome in awe—along with other transfixing moments beneath the oculus of the Pantheon, Santa Maria's golden mosaic, Michelangelo's dome in St. Peter's, and his ceiling in the Sistine Chapel.

It turns out that looking upward is actually beneficial to our overall health, and most certainly for grief, as well. The very act of looking up encourages deep breathing, decreases stress, and brings us fully into the present moment. Experiencing awe and wonder also increases our creativity and sense of connection to others.

Contemplating the limitless sky reminds us of the vastness of the Universe and offers a new perspective on our own existence. No wonder Galileo did not fear the night—or his own grief. He had glimpsed eternity and understood his place within it.

I began to see the perfection of this journey through Italy. At every step along the way I was being challenged to look within at my long-repressed grief, but I was also given the grace I needed to heal it. This too was a form of love—being guided in each moment toward my own wholeness.

After spending time in the Duomo, we followed our new tradition by joining the *passeggiata* through the historic center of Florence before finding a place for dinner. But off in the distance we heard the steady rhythm of drums, punctuated by occasional trumpet blasts, and wondered what might be happening. The other pedestrians shifted course toward the Piazza della Signoria, so we followed along, curious to see what we would find.

Soon we spotted a parade up ahead, with young people dressed in medieval and Renaissance costumes, carrying brightly colored banners, followed by rows of drummers beating a synchronized rhythm that echoed through the narrow streets. The trumpets passed next, blasting fanfares and ancient tunes. Then came the flag-throwers, who put on a dazzling display—tossing, catching, and twirling flags in perfect symmetry. We watched in delight and then joined the crowd as it wound through several more streets—laughing, clapping, and cheering with the other spectators.

We were glimpsing Florence's vibrant past, and marveled at the preservation of such authentic tradition and culture. Though we never learned the reason for that particular parade, we felt lucky to have stumbled upon it, and we knew we would not soon forget the joy and wonder in the air. Once again, Italy had surprised us when we least expected it. This exuberant display of history, art, and community revealed something deeper: here, grief is not hidden because the people instinctively know how to create containers for sorrow … and rituals for its release.

On our way back to the hotel, we found a small family-owned trattoria that seemed to call to us. I was craving something different—something that would feed my soul after this momentous day of epiphanies—so I ordered the specialty of the house, *ribollita*, not knowing what to expect.

The waiter explained that *ribollita* is a traditional Tuscan peasant dish, made from leftovers like stale bread, cooked beans, wilted greens, and vegetable scraps from previous meals.

The name literally means "reboiled," and I interpreted it as a second chance—an opportunity for new life—for food that would otherwise have been discarded.

Nothing was wasted.

Everything had been transformed to make this humble, hearty soup, finished with a swirl of peppery olive oil that filled me with comfort and warmth.

To me—sitting at a wobbly metal table in a narrow corridor outside a dimly lit café, where a family toiled together to prepare their traditional dishes for strangers—this was *grief stew*: a jumble of things left over that seemingly didn't belong anywhere else.

Neglected and devalued but still had substance to offer when simmered together by a graceful hand.

This was holy food that truly fed my soul.

Ribollita became one of my favorite dishes of the trip, and I ordered it many times afterward.

What is grief, if not a stew made from varying remnants of sorrow—changing each day in flavor and consistency—becoming tender and sacred over time …

until it tastes only of love.

This city of rebirth and Renaissance had offered me art, architecture, ancient medicine, ritual, and two of its exiled sons, Dante and Galileo—with poetry and the light of the stars.

I was gradually being shown a path out of the inferno of grief toward the presence of Divine Love.

My heart was being resurrected ... one piece at a time.

Stardust
There is a galaxy of grief
in my sky
made of stars
mysterious and uncharted
that light up the darkness
with their sparkling tears.
I look up to see
that we are all connected,
all ONE.
I am a Universe
made of stardust
and just a speck
of eternity
but I am whole
and I am LOVE.

NOVENA DAY 4

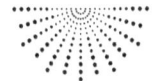

FLORENCE - CHURCH OF ORSONMICHELE

Gratitude turns what we have into enough, and more. It turns denial into acceptance, chaos into order, confusion into clarity...it makes sense of our past, brings peace for today, and creates a vision for tomorrow.

— MELODY BEATTIE

The next day began on one of Florence's most iconic sites—Ponte Vecchio, or the "old bridge"—a medieval stone crossing rebuilt in the 13th century to span the Arno River. Bridges have always played an essential role in history: enabling travel and trade, military movement and cultural exchange, and the cross-pollination of ideas. This particular bridge stands out as a lifeline of the city, once lined with butcher shops and now home to jewelers and goldsmiths.

Ponte Vecchio is also a powerful symbol of resilience and endurance, as the oldest surviving bridge in Florence—and the only one spared by the Nazis during their retreat in World War II. According to legend, a German consul and art historian stationed in Florence intervened to protect it, recognizing its historical and artistic value. During his tenure, he also helped safeguard great works of art and reportedly aided in the rescue of many Florentine Jews. Thanks to him, much of the soul and beauty of Florence was preserved.

The survival of that single bridge allowed Florence to begin its return to life after the devastation of war. Bridges are always more than stone and mortar—they span the divide between what was and what is yet to be. They create liminal spaces of transition, where grief meets resilience and sorrow gives way to the possibility of transformation. Just as we saw with St. Bonaventure—whose teachings unite the earthly and the spiritual—a bridge can be essential for life to flourish. It invites us to move forward, however precariously, because life continues to flow.

At the time, I didn't recognize the deeper meaning of starting this day on a bridge. But in hindsight, it was no accident. The lessons of this day would carry me across an inner threshold—into a new way of seeing, and a more integrated way of being.

As we toured the sites in Florence I nearly skipped the modest little church of Orsanmichele, even though my guidebook recommended it for some reason. From the description, it sounded small and a little quirky—a grain market that had been converted into a church? I was searching for a site for my next Novena prayer, and this didn't fit my expectations. After the grandeur of St. Peter's and the Duomo, it sounded too humble, too ordinary.

But then I remembered—I was not just a tourist checking off landmarks or collecting photos for social media. I was a *grief traveler*. And I had already learned that the only way to proceed on this journey was to walk slowly, intuitively—led by my senses and my heart, not my head. I needed to suspend my expectations in order to encounter what was real and what mattered.

I found Orsanmichele on a nondescript street. Again, I had to quiet the voice of my judgmental mind—the part of me still longing to orchestrate and control each moment. I stepped between the marble columns into the cool interior of the church, which was unlike the other spectacular cathedrals I had visited, yet was beautiful and soulful in its simplicity.

There was a quaintness to this fusion of the practical and the spiritual, to reimagining and reshaping a space to fulfill the needs of the community—whether hungry for grain or for spiritual solace.

As I looked around, my eyes were immediately drawn to a massive tabernacle on the right side of the space. Made of marble and inlaid with gold, it housed a painting titled *Madonna and Child with Angels*. I learned that this painting had long been associated with miraculous healings during the Black Death, eventually becoming known as the "official painting of Florence."

Pilgrims traveled from around the world to see it, to pray, to offer votives. In the image, Mary cradles the infant Jesus on her lap. He lifts his right hand to touch her cheek as she bends toward him, her gaze full of love. In his left hand, he holds a goldfinch—a symbol of joy. The way she bowed toward her son—with such tenderness, such pure love—transported me back to the *Pietà*. This was another expression of mother and child, but in a different key.

The sweetness of the moment pierced my heart. I felt tears rising —tears for all the mothers who have lost a child, and for Julio's mother in particular. That kind of grief is unspeakable. It defies measurement or containment. I could only imagine the stories of supplicants who had come here to pray to this Madonna—to offer their broken hearts, their hopes, their sorrow—during those tragic years of the plague.

Here, in this house of the ordinary—once filled with grain, now steeped in grace—I found the perfect place for a sacred Novena prayer.

I lit a candle in the hush of that space and prayed for a miracle— not the reversal of what had happened, but for the possibility of healing. I joined my heart with all those who had laid their grief open before Mary and her child, calling on the sweet countenance of the Divine Mother to hold their sorrow, to lean gently toward their gestures of love—no matter how small.

"May Julio's mother—and all grieving mothers—be shown the path that eventually leads to peace. And may I find a path to one day hold joy lightly in the palm of my hand again."

This was the fourth Novena prayer—spoken in a house that had once held grain and now held miracles—for Julio's mother, and for all who bear the unbearable. I paused for a moment to try to remember the last time I felt pure, unbridled joy ... but I couldn't recall the feeling itself ... or when I had experienced it.

I had traded away my joy for safety ... for control ... for survival.

And I was so very weary of living without joy.

From Orsanmichele and the loving embrace of the Divine Mother, we entered the busy central pedestrian street of Florence, where market stalls once bustled and now tourists and mothers pushing strollers mingled with people in business suits and clerics in long robes.

I was gradually learning to trust the process of this journey with grief and to follow my intuition with each step. We turned onto a quiet side street to escape the throngs and allow time for more exploration. The smell of freshly baked bread and espresso filled the air, along with the sound of dishes clattering in small sidewalk cafés, calling us to stop for a cappuccino break.

Again, I was met with the ordinary—the day-to-day existence—where grief is truly lived and carried, or rejected and buried. I recognized once more that my grief over Julio's death had opened the floodgates of long-repressed pain—and guilt—that I had avoided for so many years after my father's death. This was an opportunity to finally face it, and I prayed for the strength and presence to do so.

We continued our walk and after tracing the edges of medieval Florence, the road began to widen as the Basilica of Santa Croce rose before us, gleaming with green and white marble like the Duomo. I had come to see the final resting places of Galileo and Michelangelo, whose artistry and sorrow-laden stories had become companions on this pilgrimage of grief.

But before entering, I was drawn to a towering statue of Dante on the steps leading to the church. Created for the 600th anniversary of the poet's birth, the sculpture shows him holding *The Divine Comedy*, with an eagle at his feet.

Dante, one of the beloved sons of Florence as we saw before, died in exile in Ravenna where he is buried, but the city still mourns his absence—as shown by this statue and the empty tomb created for him inside the basilica. These are tangible reminders of a poignant truth: grief is amplified when we fail to reconcile our differences during the fleeting span of life.

Inside, I found the tomb of Galileo—another exiled son of Florence—who was initially denied burial in the basilica due to condemnation by the Church. A century later, when the world finally recognized the truth of his contributions to science, this tomb was created to honor him.

His daughter, Sister Maria Celeste, was secretly buried with him —placed there by a devoted student who wished to reunite father and daughter in death. The tomb features a bust of Galileo with a telescope in hand, gazing toward the heavens. Two statues, representing Astronomy and Geometry, flank the sarcophagus. It is a fitting tribute to the man who set the stage for Newton, and who suffered for seeing what the world could not.

Directly across from Galileo lies Michelangelo, who died just days after Galileo's birth. Some say the artist's spirit entered the newborn astronomer—as if genius can be passed like a torch.

Who can say how brilliance is born or nurtured on this planet?

All we know is that it endures exile and loss—and somehow still blooms.

Just like love.

Michelangelo's tomb is magnificent, befitting a man whose contributions to art and architecture shaped a nation. A bust of the artist sits high at the center, while three grieving figures—representing Painting, Sculpture, and Architecture—gather around the sarcophagus.

As with Galileo, controversy surrounded his burial. Michelangelo died in Rome, in self-imposed exile to protest the rule of Alessandro de' Medici in Florence. His body was buried in Rome, but his nephew was dispatched to steal the corpse and return it to Florence, where it arrived hidden in a bale of hay. According to legend, when the coffin was opened, Michelangelo's body had not decayed—causing some to view him as a saint.

Michelangelo's creativity was born of pain, but it was becoming clear to me that my own pain—left unacknowledged—had stifled my creativity and suffocated my joy. Repressed grief leads to its own kind of suffering: a numb, isolated emptiness, like viewing life through cloudy glass—always reaching for what looks like happiness, but never able to touch it.

I learned from the guidebook that Santa Croce had once been damaged by a horrific flood in 1966, along with many works of art throughout the city. In early November of that year, a convergence of events led to the most devastating flood in the history of the Arno River.

One-third of Florence's annual rainfall fell in just two days. Low-pressure systems and heavy storms in northern Italy caused rivers across Tuscany to swell. Hydroelectric dams began releasing water into the Arno to prevent collapse. Meanwhile, the river backed up at the Ponte Vecchio, unable to push through its narrow arches. Eventually, the Arno overflowed its banks, rising as high as twenty feet in some places.

Santa Croce was particularly vulnerable because it had been built on marshland lower than the river itself. The church—and seventy percent of the city—was inundated with water, mud, and fuel oil from broken motors and heaters. Many people lost their lives and homes. Countless artworks, manuscripts, and books were damaged. Today, markers on the church's outer walls still show how high the waters rose—above the main doors.

But miraculously, the world responded. Florence was beloved internationally for its artistic treasures, and scholars rushed in to help. Working together, they developed new methods for removing oil from delicate surfaces. Volunteers—nicknamed "mud angels"—came from all over the globe and worked tirelessly to rescue and restore whatever they could.

It was a devastating tragedy. But Florence was no stranger to loss. This city had always found a way to carry on, sometimes with the help of angels who thrive in the mud.

@

After leaving the church we crossed the Arno at the nearest bridge—Ponte alle Grazie, the Bridge of Grace and Gratitude—a fitting metaphor for what I had been learning that day. At the center of the bridge lies a memorial site where, each year, the city holds a ceremony to remember the victims of the flood. Wreaths are dropped into the water, words are spoken, tears are shed.

I stood at that site and held my own remembrance ritual, dropping a small flower I'd picked from the riverbank into the flowing current, just as I had done in Rome a few days before.

As I watched the flower float away, the thought occurred to me that this was the bridge of Gratitude, which rises from the plain of Grief and allows us to reach the other side where perhaps Joy can be found. We simply have to find a way to cross the bridge— to experience gratitude for whatever life has offered us.

In that moment I received a message. Five words arrived, like a gift. I pulled out my little travel journal and wrote them down immediately: Life, Love, Laughter, Loss, Longing.

They were the Five Gratitudes. Perhaps they were the secret to "crossing the bridge" and finding joy on the other side.

I paused, looking down at the page. The first gratitude was for Life. Yes—even in the midst of so much death and destruction, I could feel deep thankfulness for simply being alive. To be standing there at that moment, on the Bridge of Grace and Gratitude.

"Thank you for Life."

Glancing at my husband, I felt overwhelmed with appreciation for his care, his companionship, his patience—for walking beside me on this romantic getaway turned grief pilgrimage. He was there with me, even though the sorrow was not his to carry. That is love.

"Thank you for Love."

I remembered how the music and dancing during the Rosh Hashanah dinner in Rome stirred us to make a toast and join the revelry; and how good it felt to laugh at our drenched reflections in the mirror after being caught in the downpour the day before.

"Thank you for Laughter."

But I hesitated when I reached the fourth word. Loss. It felt counterintuitive. Grief doesn't usually lead us toward gratitude—it pulls us into regret and despair. Where could thanks be found in the midst of pain? I didn't have an answer yet. But I said the words anyway.

"Thank you for Loss."

Then came the final word: Longing. I wasn't sure I understood it. Longing for what? Did I mishear the message? I felt uneasy repeating it, uncertain of its meaning. But again, I followed the intuition I had received.

"Thank you for Longing."

Only later would I begin to understand. This inspiration wasn't asking me to find gratitude *in spite of* loss, but *because* of it. I was just beginning to glimpse the truth: that loss deepens us. It softens the soul. It is the floodwater through which transformation becomes possible. We descend into the mud of grief, and it is from that very mud that we begin to rise—with new insight, new clarity, new compassion.

And for that, I was—indeed—grateful.

But that last word stayed with me: longing.

At the time, I didn't yet know where it was leading me. I only knew something had been stirring deep within me—an ache I hadn't named. A longing for completion. A longing for growth. A longing, perhaps, for the miracle I had prayed for that morning.

I couldn't see it clearly yet.

But maybe—just maybe—it was already happening.

While I continued to ponder these Five Gratitudes, we left the Grazie Bridge and began to stroll through Oltrarno: "the other side of the Arno." We found it to be charming—less touristy and much quieter than the historic center of Florence. There were artisan shops and art galleries everywhere, a continuation from the days of the Renaissance when this neighborhood was a hub for creatives, including Leonardo da Vinci and Michelangelo.

We made our way up a steep hill and eventually arrived at Piaz-zale Michelangelo—a wide terrace with a sweeping panoramic view of Florence that took our breath away. Across the Arno River, we could see the Duomo rising up majestically, the Ponte Vecchio, the Uffizi Gallery, and the Basilica of Santa Croce, which we had visited earlier that day.

While we were sightseeing in the city, we couldn't quite get our bearings—tall buildings and winding streets left us feeling slightly disoriented. But this view from above brought clarity to the map of Florence. From this vantage point, we could trace our own footsteps and also understand the relationships between all the places we had visited—how they interconnected, geographi-cally as well as historically.

I didn't recognize it then, but I see now how our spiritual journeys are so much like that. While we're in the midst of our experiences, we feel dazed and lost—we cannot get a clear picture of what is happening to us (or for us). But later, when we've had time to ascend a bit and catch our breath, we can see it all from a new perspective. The connections become apparent. The journey begins to make more sense, even if it still feels mysterious and serendipitous. That day, I was simply grateful for the view from above—and for a new way of seeing.

Further up the hill, we saw an interesting church. It hadn't been on our list of sights to see, but it somehow drew us in. There was a different look and feel to this place: the Church of San Miniato al Monte. This beautiful structure was built during the Romanesque period, after the fall of the Roman Empire but before the extraordinary Renaissance had begun in Florence.

That era was once called the "Dark Ages," when many Roman advancements were thought to have been lost—such as the knowledge needed to build something like the Pantheon. But we now know that this term was misleading. The era had its own rich legacy, and San Miniato is a stunning example of the architectural brilliance of that time.

One of the features that makes San Miniato so unique is the use of sacred geometry throughout the structure, which contributes to its energy—its soul of place—and explains why we felt drawn to explore further. The church's façade is composed of precise geometric shapes, triangles and rectangles, stacked in harmonious symmetry.

But what intrigued me most was what I found inside: a large zodiac circle, inlaid in marble at the center of the sanctuary floor. It was deliberately aligned with the path of the sun.

The windows in the walls above the nave were also constructed with celestial precision, designed to direct sunbeams and shadows across the church at specific times of the year. During the summer solstice, for example, a circular beam of sunlight illuminates the Cancer symbol on the zodiac floor. And during Easter, the mosaic above the altar—depicting Christ and the Virgin Mary—is lit from behind by sunlight at just the right angle.

We read about many other solar and lunar alignments built into this church with care and intention. Then we sat for hours, watching the sunbeams dance along the stones, tracing soft patterns across the sanctuary. I was mesmerized. It was astonishing to realize that centuries ago, architects had the skill and insight to design something so complex, so attuned to the heavens.

The sacred geometry had a calming, illuminating effect on me. It whispered of a divine order and celestial timing that quietly hold the universe together. I felt connected to those ancient souls who had also tried to make sense of the cosmos, to see the invisible networks and threads that connect us. Once again, I felt held. Seen. Contained in something loving.

Feeling calm and accepting after my time in the sanctuary, I walked outside into the Cemetery of the Holy Doors—Porte Sante—which was built much more recently than the basilica. I wandered among the headstones for which this hillside burial site is known, perched high above Florence and the Arno River.

I saw a life-size sculpture of a young man and a young woman holding hands; a mother with four small children at her feet; and another of a grieving man sprawled across the top of a grave. Yes —the grief along this Earthbound part of the journey is palpable and overwhelming. It was everywhere I looked, inescapable—because it is such an essential part of life. That truth was becoming very clear to me.

But a little farther on, I was stunned by the sight of a contemporary sculpture in the center of the square. It turned out to be on temporary loan from the Korean sculptor Park Eun Sun. The name of the piece translated literally to "Infinite Column Increasing."

It was an inverted funnel-shaped structure made of alternating layers of granite and marble, stacked one upon another. As the column rose upward and widened, the layers became slightly displaced and asymmetrical. Cracks had formed along the spiral —circling up and down the surface like a winding fracture line.

At the midpoint, a full break split the structure horizontally, yet it remained somehow intact—conveying a sense of imperfect, continuous growth.

A thought struck me: this sculpture was an extraordinary depiction of consciousness expanding over time. There are breaks and imperfections—discontinuities in the process— but growth continues. According to the artist, the cracks and holes allow us to glimpse the interior, while also letting the inside grow along with the outside. These openings create a dialogue between full and empty, high and low, heaven and earth, human and cosmos, wild and holy.

I read these words while standing in the cemetery plaza, and once again, I was inspired by what I discovered. This sculpture— coincidentally on loan here, on the very day I felt drawn to San Miniato and wandered into the cemetery—embodied everything I had been experiencing and witnessing during my time in Florence.

I had learned of the devastation of the plague, the great flood and its mud angels, the transcendence of the Renaissance, and now this reminder of continuous, uneven growth. Consciousness doesn't stop. It keeps rising—even through the fractures, even when everything feels displaced or out of balance. It takes energy to reorient, to hold things together, but the cracks don't destroy the growth. They shape it.

This broken, spiraled, gorgeous column became a final emblem of all I had felt during those two days. I was beginning to see more clearly that I needed to allow the imperfections and flaws— the breaks, the losses, the pain that come with being alive. To embrace the suffering and longing is the only way toward healing and growth. It all happens together—it's all part of the same process.

I understood, more clearly than ever before, that resisting the pain of grief over my father's death and the loss of my patient would only cause me to shrink, to harden, to stop expanding. Avoidance leads to stagnation. But surrendering to grief, letting it flow through me, would open the way for growth and even transcendence.

This visit to Florence had allowed me to immerse myself more fully into grief and sorrow—but also more fully into beauty, joy, and celebration. Living and loving every aspect of life. Seeing everything. Taking it all in. Holding it lightly. And at last, feeling a quiet, holy gratitude for all of it.

Following our visit to San Miniato and the cemetery, we walked back downhill to Piazzale Michelangelo. The sky had begun to shift as the sun descended—soft pinks, then gold, then a deepening indigo. We found a kiosk selling gelato on the terrace, and I chose a cup of pistachio and hazelnut—sweet, earthy, simple.

Standing at the overlook, surrounded by tourists who were unusually quiet, we watched the sun's sinking rays illuminate the city across the river. The dome, the towers, the streets winding like threads through time—all lit up in the path of the sun. Florence had endured plague, floods, rebirth, revolution. And still, here it was—glowing beneath a dying sun, alive with passion and creativity.

I tasted the melting gelato and thought about the preciousness of things that are impermanent—those that dissolve in our hands even as we reach for them. Maybe this present moment is the purpose of all of it—a quiet sunset, a city that has survived, sweetness mingled with sorrow. And me, learning—one revelation at a time—how to taste the joy of life again.

Grateful
I am the lotus growing in the mud
the phoenix rising from the ashes
the fractured column growing infinitely
from ground toward the cosmos.
And I am also
mud
and ash
and ground
reaching down
to gather what has been lost
and upward toward stars
that whisper
of Love
and Grace.
And I am grateful for all of it.

NOVENA DAY 5

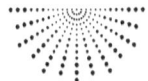

MONTEROSSO AL MARE - CHURCH OF ST. JOHN THE BAPTIST

Those who contemplate the beauty of the earth find reserves of strength that will endure as long as life lasts. There is something infinitely healing in the repeated refrains of nature—the assurance that dawn comes after night, and spring after winter.

— RACHEL CARSON

The next morning, we awoke early for a journey I had been looking forward to for months. We were heading to Cinque Terre along the Ligurian Sea. Cinque Terre—"the five lands" in Italian—refers to five medieval villages, each nestled in a ravine or perched on a hilltop overlooking the water. Historically, these communities were connected only by sea or footpath; even today, each village retains its distinct dialect and heritage. Though close in proximity, hiking from one village to the next was once grueling—steep, rugged trails made travel difficult, so the towns remained largely separate.

Each village started out with a hilltop castle, and from there homes were built below, cascading downward toward the sea. Over the centuries, these towns were repeatedly attacked by pirates who landed on their beaches or piers, intending to loot and destroy. When danger came, villagers fled uphill to seek refuge behind castle walls.

Along the coast, watchtowers were built in line-of-sight to one another. A fire lit in one tower signaled the next, and then the next, until the warning had reached every town. For centuries, this is how these communities looked out for one another—protecting each other from the ravages of the sea and the cruelty of strangers.

I had seen photos of Cinque Terre's quiet charm, and that's why I was so eager to go. Even though it's more touristy now, it still feels serene compared to the bustle of Rome or Florence.

We traveled from Florence by train, but—as journeys go— we got off at the wrong station and missed our high-speed connection to Monterosso al Mare, where we were staying. Instead, we found ourselves stranded for several hours, then placed on the slow train—a regional line that moved sluggishly and stopped at every tiny town along the way.

But for this journey of grief, the slow train turned out to be a blessing.

Grief needs time and space to breathe, to move freely, to surface and speak.

At that unhurried pace, I had hours to reflect, journal, and process the previous four days. I also got to confront my frustration at not being able to control the schedule—and in a small act of surrender, I put away my meticulously detailed trip spreadsheet. Grief doesn't care about itineraries. It has its own holy logic, its own timing. And while the mind tries to orchestrate special moments, it's often the ordinary ones—the delays, detours, and quiet pauses—that offer the most transformation.

@

After winding through dark mountain tunnels for what felt like hours, we finally emerged into the afternoon sunshine. Waking from a coma must feel something like that: from endless darkness into radiant sun. Below us stretched the Ligurian Sea. Above it, pastel-colored buildings clung to cliff walls—stacked like coral against the sky, rising impossibly from stone. My frustration vanished ... it was breathtaking.

Our hotel was in Monterosso al Mare, the northernmost village, which meant our slow train passed through all five towns along the way. It was a perfect opportunity to absorb the beauty: slowly.

This is something Italians understand that we Americans often forget—**good things take time**. Food, wine, friendship, art, sex— and yes, even grief—are meant to be savored. Here on this unplanned pilgrimage, I was learning to slow down and receive it all.

Old Town Monterosso is medieval in character, with narrow cobbled streets, archways, and no cars—just footsteps and laughter echoing off stone. The vibrant buildings spilled down to the beach, many crumbling in places, but all overflowing with life: flower boxes, bougainvillea, laundry flapping from windows, patios stacked on top of one another like children's blocks.

To reach our hotel, we climbed steep paths and dozens of stairs. The lobby sat high on the hillside and opened onto a panoramic view of the sea. Our hosts—whose family had run the hotel for generations—greeted us with glasses of *sciacchetrà*, the sweet wine of the region. We felt like we had come home.

Our room had a small patio nestled beside the hotel's garden, where they grew herbs, wildflowers, and a small orchard of lemon and olive trees. It was wonderful to be so close to the Earth again—to feel its pulse and remember that healing often begins in the body.

There wasn't much sightseeing to do, and that was perfect. I spent what seemed like hours sitting at a little wrought-iron table in the garden—bathing in the scent of thyme and lemon, running my fingers over the leathery leaves of the olive tree, listening to waves and distant laughter and the clinking of wine glasses. I watched the sunlight shimmer across the Ligurian Sea and let it wash over me like a blessing.

It was a feast for the senses. A place outside of time. And exactly what I needed.

@

Later that afternoon we took a self-guided walking tour through Monterosso's Old Town that led us up a steep hill to the village cemetery. I've long been drawn to cemeteries and wanted a quiet stroll among the gravesites. You can learn a lot about a place by how it honors its dead.

Because of its perch high above the town, the cemetery offered the best view in all of Monterosso. From there, I could see the curve of the coastline stretching in both directions, with the other four villages of Cinque Terre dotting the hillsides in the distance. Above them, terraced vineyards and gardens climbed toward the sky—testimony to the ancient bond between people and land.

Each of the five villages has its own hilltop cemetery and a sanctuary dedicated to Mary. Though close in proximity, they are fiercely independent and self-sustaining—distinct in dialect, heritage, and rhythm of life. Like siblings who grow up side by side yet develop entirely different identities.

Inside the cemetery was a wall of marble *loculi*—rectangular burial niches, each one holding a coffin or an urn, sealed with a carved plaque. Names, birth and death dates, and always a small oval portrait in black and white are featured, along with a vase for flowers and a tiny electric light.

Most niches were adorned with fresh blooms, and many of the photographs showed faces weathered by sea and sun. These were the people of the village below—fishermen, farmers, shopkeepers—who had lived their entire lives on this rugged edge between land and sea.

I paused in silence, touched by the intimacy of it all. These were ordinary lives, and yet something sacred emanated from the care with which they had been remembered. Their bodies now rested in stone, just as their lives had been shaped by it—stones worn smooth by salt air, hands hardened by labor, hearts softened by kinship.

When someone dies at home in Cinque Terre, tradition and law require the family to keep the body there for one to two days. The entire village comes to call. It's a custom from centuries past, still lovingly preserved in these coastal hamlets. In a world rushing toward speed and efficiency, this slow ritual of presence stands as a profound act of reverence. The people here have survived for generations by bonding tightly in community—through feast and famine, storm and sunshine, life and death.

O n a terrace just beyond the cemetery stood a bronze statue of St. Francis of Assisi overlooking the sea. He leaned gently toward a wolf, his right hand resting lightly on the creature's head, his left hand lifted in a gesture of peace toward the heavens. The wolf, in turn, offered a raised paw. It was a tender rendering of the old legend from Gubbio, where Francis calmed a vicious wolf through the power of love and presence.

The message was unmistakable.

Francis—gentle saint, lover of all wild things—presides over Monterosso al Mare as a symbol of harmony. His compassion embraces not just beasts and villagers, but the sea itself, source of both livelihood and loss for those below.

And here I was, standing in a village suspended between earth and water, life and death, anchored by memory and mercy. I felt myself growing quieter inside—less afraid of endings, more attuned to what endures.

C ontinuing our walking tour around Monterosso's Old Town, we learned more of the region's history and folklore. The stories were sobering: storms and shipwrecks, fishermen lost at sea, invaders who once slaughtered entire populations, and the pillboxes of World War II—concrete outposts the Germans built along the coast to watch for Allied ships and submarines.

This has always been a hard place to live—clinging to cliffs above the sea, navigating steep cobbled streets day after day, enduring suffering, hardship, and loss. And yet, the beauty here is undeniable. The vitality of the natural world pulses through everything: lemon trees, cascading flowers, the turquoise sea. The people, like the land, are weathered and resilient. You can sense that their spirits are sustained not only by endurance, but by the soul of this wild, isolated place.

As we wandered the quiet alleys, I began looking for just the right place for my next Novena prayer. This one would be different. For the first time, I felt I could carry the weight of sorrow and still take in the beauty around me—no longer crushed beneath grief, but carrying it with me.

I found a small square in front of the Church of St. John the Baptist. A high-water mark from the devastating 1966 flood—the same one that struck Florence—was still visible on the stone walls. Back then, torrents of mud had poured through the ravine and damaged much of Monterosso. But the little church remained, bearing witness.

Above the door, an elegant rose window glowed with late-afternoon light. I stepped inside and found a quiet, humble sanctuary. A triptych depicting the Madonna and Child between two saints caught my eye. This would be the place.

I lit a small votive and said the prayer:

"May Julio's family experience relief from their sorrow and begin to see the light of hope. Help me learn to hold the precious balance between sorrow and joy without needing to control it."

After a time of silent reflection, I stepped back into the square—and found myself facing another church directly across from the first. It was smaller and more mysterious, with a striped black-and-white marble façade. Above the door, an hourglass and a skull and crossbones had been carved into the stone. It was named the Oratory of the Dead, which immediately caught my attention.

Inside, the stucco decorations and frescoes depicted skeletons and skulls, serving as a reminder of the fleeting nature of life.. I learned this church was the home of the Brotherhood of Death and Prayer, a confraternity that arranges funerals for less fortunate individuals, cares for widows and orphans, and honors strangers who had shipwrecked at sea.

It was a gift of love and dignity, offered freely to the dead and grieving.

I stood there in silence, touched by this sacred work. My heart ached suddenly for Julio's family—would they be able to afford a funeral for him? I remembered how they came to our clinic for help, how limited their resources had been. I longed for there to be a Brotherhood like this in our town to look after besieged families, to lead them gently through the sacred rituals, and ask for nothing in return.

Another prayer surfaced:

"Make sure they receive the help they need."

But as soon as I whispered it, I remembered the friar in Rome, his kind eyes and gentle nod. The reassurance he offered had echoed through every Novena prayer since. I felt the answer rise quietly within me:

It is already done.

Like the square that connects these sister churches—one for the living and one for the dead— I was standing in a liminal space, traveling between worlds, between my roles as caregiver and griever, daughter and doctor; between my years of hidden grief and my unfolding transformation; between sorrow and joy, the wild and the holy.

That night, exhausted and hungry, we found a tiny café tucked into a narrow alley. I ordered ravioli stuffed with pear and ricotta. The first bite stopped me—it was a sacred experience, a moment of flavor and light.

Larry tried to order seafood pasta in Italian and ended up with grilled fish instead, which caused us both to break out laughing. But he loved it! In fact, grilled fish became one of his favorite entrees, and he ordered it again and again in the days that followed. Laughter and wine and a lovingly prepared meal go a long way to soothe the sorrows of any day.

This spiritual journey we're all on—whether we know it or not—is so strange and beautiful. Most of it appears chaotic with brief moments of sublime glory in between agonizing stretches of confusion, darkness and pain.

We get what we don't want and then something we haven't thought to ask for arrives before we know we need it. It seems there is no sense to it all—and yet—there are moments when you can see so clearly that everything is connected and everything is working on your behalf, no matter how challenging.

Those glimpses can come more frequently when we are diligent on the path, embracing the challenges, letting go of our expectations, but this is rough grace.

It can take everything we have to keep going, but that is what life asks us to do.

I awoke early the next morning, after my first night of deep, restful sleep since I'd learned that Julio had died. Jet lag was finally lifting—but so was the grief insomnia that had haunted me since the news. I couldn't have been more relieved.

The sun was just beginning to rise over the Ligurian hills. I stepped out onto our garden patio to meditate and write in my journal. After so many days of movement, this was a welcome pause—a quiet space for stillness and solitude.

Carla, the owner of the inn, appeared from around the corner with a little tray in her hands. She brought me a frothy cappuccino and a slice of whole wheat toast with homemade lemon marmalade— made from the very lemons growing on the tree above my head.

I sat there in the delicate light of early morning, inhaling the scent of lemon and thyme, and tasting the bittersweet marmalade on my tongue.

And I wrote.

I wrote about the grief I could finally name—still tender in my heart—but no longer buried. I wrote about waking up to feel a flicker of joy. Something was shifting. I had made progress over the past week, and the Novena prayers were helping me. At last, I was beginning to taste the sweetness of life again.

And I was learning something essential: the bitter and the sweet live side by side.

One deepens the other.

They cannot—and should not—be separated.

That realization arrived just in time. Today we would embark on the long-awaited hike across all five villages of the Cinque Terre, a journey we'd been anticipating for months. Our path followed ancient trails that once formed a lifeline between these cliffside towns—long before roads and trains connected them.

We climbed steep stone steps through terraced gardens filled with olive and lemon trees. Stone walls gave way to wild bougainvillea spilling magenta over gates and fences. We crossed narrow bridges and rocky outcroppings, with the hillside rising to our left and the vast Ligurian Sea unfurling far below on our right.

We stopped in each village along the way—Vernazza, Corniglia, Manarola—for water and snacks, for glimpses into the soul of each place. Though geographically close, each village had its own rhythm, its own memory, its own love affair with the sea.

Between Manarola and Riomaggiore, we reached a portion of the trail known as the Via dell'Amore—the Path of Love. Carved into the cliffs with sweeping views of the water, it had once been a meeting place for lovers from the two towns, separated by geography but united by longing.

Along the trail, a metal arch held two hearts at its center, over-flowing with padlocks—left by couples over the years as symbols of enduring love.

We stopped to embrace in that sacred place where generations had once met. And in that moment, I remembered why we had come: to celebrate our love.

Grief had reshaped the journey, yes—but love had always been the reason for it.

As we approached the outskirts of Riomaggiore, we stumbled upon a cliffside bar perched impossibly above the sea. It looked like it had been suspended in air. We decided to stop, rest our tired legs, and order a glass of wine. The wind carried sea mist onto our cheeks as we clinked our glasses and toasted this magical day.

We stayed longer than we intended, letting the beauty of it all wash over us. The roar of the sea, the sweetness of the wine, the hush of having done something meaningful with our time.

Eventually we realized we were late for the ferry back to Monterosso. We leapt up and ran laughing through the winding streets, reaching the jetty just as the captain was pulling up the stairs to the boat.

Out of breath and smiling, we climbed aboard. In that moment, I felt completely alive—free, lighthearted, and fully in the flow of life.

And it was wonderful.

On our last night in Monterosso—after a day spent hiking the narrow trails that stitch the five villages together—we sat down to our most elegant meal of the journey. It felt like a celebration. Not just of the day's beauty, but of something more subtle and precious: the glimmer of joy that had re-entered my heart.

There was a lightness between us again, a reconnection now that some of the heaviness had lifted. Perhaps, finally, our "second honeymoon" was beginning.

We started with anchovies—*acciughe*, as they're called in Italian. I had never eaten one before and was skeptical I'd enjoy them. But everyone we met in the Cinque Terre insisted: you must try the anchovies—freshly caught that very morning in the waters just below our feet.

They arrived nestled in a sauce of tomatoes, olive oil, and capers —delicate and briny, full of flavor and life. I took a cautious bite and was stunned. I had discovered something new to love—an unexpected delight.

Next came the seafood risotto. It was presented in a wide copper pot for sharing, sealed under a golden crust of baked dough. We broke it open together, releasing a fragrant puff of steam that smelled like the salt air of the sea.

Beneath the crust lay a bed of warm, creamy risotto, stirred slowly for hours and infused with the tenderness of the morning's catch. The flavor was indescribable.

We ate slowly, reverently, closing our eyes to savor each bite.

Maybe it was the crashing waves just beyond, the fatigue in my body from our long hike, the lemon trees nearby perfuming the air, the chill of the white wine in my hand—but something about that meal fed me in a way I had never known. It satisfied even the hunger of my soul.

It felt like a breakthrough.

Here, in this land of cliffs and color—where pastel houses cling to stone like prayers, where the sea has delivered both livelihood and loss, where storms and shipwrecks and sorrow are etched into every surface—I found it.

I found the taste of joy I had longed for since my father's death.

Here, amidst the hardship and resilience of this place, I discovered that joy can survive even when grief floods the heart.

That it is possible to hold a sliver of solace, even in the shadow of sorrow.

More than halfway through the pilgrimage now, I felt something in me exhale. The sea had softened me. The trail had steadied me. And the soul of this place had reminded me that beauty always finds a way to remain.

Relaxed, restored, and deeply nourished, I looked forward to what the next day might bring.

Resilience

There is a harsh grace
suspended on craggy cliffs
between sea and sky
swept by salt air
and tides that bring
life one day
and death the next.
Resilience is woven
into DNA and
infused in the marrow.
Grief cloaks the shoulders
from the bitter breeze
but joy pushes
through every crack
until it reaches the stars.
And there is so much
necessary forgiveness
to navigate
this hard
and vibrant life.
And so it is …
the rough grace
of grief
that can no longer
be hidden.

NOVENA DAY 6

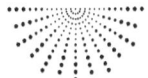

SIENA - ORATORY OF ST. CATHERINE OF THE NIGHT

Only when we are brave enough to explore the darkness will we discover the infinite power of our light.

— BRENÉ BROWN

We left behind Monterosso al Mare on an early morning train, bound for Siena with a transfer in Empoli. Carla, ever thoughtful, had packed food for the journey: hardboiled eggs, fresh bread, cheese, and oranges from her orchard. I felt a tug of longing as the coastline disappeared—part of me wanted to linger in that sun- and sea-swept landscape that had awakened joy in my heart again. But it was time to continue the journey.

The rhythmic motion of the train lulled me to sleep near the end of the route, and when I awoke, something felt off. It took a few minutes to realize what had triggered that uneasy sensation: the outer pocket of my purse was unzipped. My stomach sank. I looked inside and discovered that my cash and credit cards were gone, along with my driver's license. Someone had stolen them from me while I slept, my purse left unguarded.

Losing cash and credit cards on a foreign trip was a serious issue —our survival depended on them to pay for food and lodging in the days ahead. My sense of safety was suddenly stripped away, along with any lingering illusion that I was in control of this journey.

That event marked the beginning of a hard fall into despair.

The joy of Monterosso dissolved instantly, as if it had only been on loan. I plunged back into grief and darkness. I had been temporarily lulled by that glimmer of joy in Cinque Terre, convinced that I had broken through, completed the arc, and arrived.

But this was a reminder that the path through grief and spiritual transformation is not linear—it is a spiral that moves both upward and downward. I was being broken open all over again.

The light I had touched was real, but incomplete.

Now I was being invited to go deeper—to shine awareness on the heavy wound of guilt that still lived within me.

The skies over Siena were heavy with dark, threatening clouds as we made our way from the train station in intermittent rain. We dragged our suitcases over uneven cobblestones, climbed steep lanes, and crossed narrow piazzas, searching for our hotel—and becoming hopelessly lost.

We needed to reach our room quickly to call the credit card companies and report the theft. But we also had only a small amount of cash—nowhere near enough to complete the trip. My anxiety mounted as we wandered, tired and soaked, trying to hold it together.

Eventually we found our bed and breakfast: a large family home with a few extra rooms for guests. The daughter, who spoke English, wasn't there to check us in, and we struggled to explain our situation to her father. He didn't seem to understand the urgency of what we were saying. He just smiled, motioning gently with his hands and repeating, "It's okay. It's okay."

After finding an ATM nearby, we managed to withdraw as much cash as possible before canceling the credit cards. But I felt disoriented and frantic. And underneath it all, guilt was rising fast.

Why had I fallen asleep? Why hadn't I been more careful with my purse?

I couldn't yet see that this self-blame was an echo of a deeper and far older guilt: the guilt of not being good enough to prevent bad things from happening ... including death.

It was guilt without logic, without answer.

Guilt that couldn't be resolved with an ATM.

I felt blindsided. Set up, almost. The joy I had experienced in Monterosso—the sacred light, the sensuality of nature, the feeling of being present and alive—had led me to believe I was through the worst. But it had been a mirage, a brief rise before the fall. And now I was devastated by my own disappointment.

Much later I would learn about the stages of the archetypal Hero's Journey as described by Joseph Campbell—stages that closely mirror the "healer's journey" I had begun to imagine for myself. Just before the hero enters the deepest depths, the story often includes a false victory—a moment of success that makes the hero believe the battle is over.

But then comes the plunge. The true darkness. The soul's descent into the cave where her deepest fears and shadows await.

Siena was my threshold.

And the stolen wallet was the harbinger of my true descent into grief.

We toured Siena the next day under skies that had brightened slightly, although my inner landscape remained dim. I was in a dark mood, but even so, I couldn't help appreciating the haunting, brooding beauty of the city.

Built around the oval-shaped Piazza del Campo, the old city's buildings and streets are formed from reddish-brown bricks made of the very soil of this hilltop. I realized that this was the namesake of my favorite childhood crayon color: Burnt Sienna— warm and earthy like autumn leaves.

There is a soothing quality to the uniform appearance of these structures, a kind of visual harmony. But there is also weight. The bricks feel heavy and that weight is palpable as you walk the narrow lanes. The soul of this place is somber—almost sorrowful —and it mirrored my mood perfectly.

. . .

Though I didn't yet fully understand my own darkness that day, I began to learn about the history of Siena—and why it felt so different from Rome and Florence.

Until 1348, Siena had been a thriving city-state, a major banking and trade center with its own army and growing influence. It rivaled Florence, Genoa, and Pisa.

But when the Black Death swept through Europe that year, it devastated Siena in particular. Nearly half the population perished. The city was brought to its knees, and unlike Florence, it never recovered.

There was no Renaissance in Siena.

While Florence rose from the ashes of plague with an explosion of art and innovation—thanks to a fortuitous convergence of creative minds and wealthy patrons—Siena remained frozen.

The social fabric was too frayed to be mended, and there was neither energy nor support for rebirth. The city became suspended in time—still Medieval, still marked by its loss.

And here I was, in Siena—a city stilled by its own devastation—descending once again into my own frozen depths. But beautiful, brooding Siena had something to teach me.

Lessons I couldn't yet see.

We walked through Il Campo, the clamshell-shaped piazza at the heart of the city, and made our way toward Siena's Gothic cathedral—the Duomo. Along the way, colorful flags and banners flew from every building, even from the balconies and windows of private apartments.

We learned that Siena is divided into seventeen *contrade*, or neighborhoods, each a fierce rival of the others—a tradition that dates back to Medieval times. Each *contrada* proudly displays its colors and mascot, and local shops brim with bandanas and flags for every allegiance.

T he cathedral itself is stunning—an architectural marvel that took over 175 years to complete. Inside are intricate mosaics and sculptures, including a statue of St. Catherine of Siena, whose story would captivate me later.

In a bold moment of ambition, Siena once tried to expand this very cathedral to compete with—and even surpass—the Duomo of Florence. Grand plans were drawn to double its size, and construction began in 1347.

But within a year, the Black Death struck. The project was abandoned, and the unfinished wall of the facade still stands today—a permanent monument to devastation and unfulfilled dreams.

Grief and guilt, frozen in stone.

M odern engineers say the cathedral never could have been completed, even in the best of times. The terrain was too unstable. The vision was too vast.

The contrast between Siena and Florence is striking. Florence, bolstered by fortune and the right minds at the right time, witnessed the miracle of Brunelleschi's dome—a dream made real against all odds. Siena, by contrast, was left with a hollow promise and a fractured foundation.

But the unfinished wall—known as the *Facciatone*—is more than a symbol of failure. Standing atop it, we discovered breathtaking views of the city in every direction. It became clear that this wall, this relic of sorrow, had become something else: a place of perspective.

A silent testament to what might have been.

A platform from which to see what is.

There is humility and courage in allowing an unfinished wall to remain—a visible scar that says: something was lost here, and we will not look away. Maybe that's why Siena became the place where I could safely go deeper into my own grief and guilt. In Siena, grief is still visible. It hasn't been torn down or buried. It's simply... there. And in its presence, something new becomes possible.

I was there to do the same: to unearth my sorrow, let it rise to the surface, and allow it to be seen.

@

On further wanderings through the somber streets of Siena, I was introduced to Saint Catherine—the pride of the city and one of the patron saints of Italy. She was born here and lived her entire life not as a nun, but as a layperson.

She didn't learn to read or write until adulthood, yet she dedicated her life to serving others with fierce devotion. Born just before the first onslaught of the Black Death, her entire life was shaped by its shadow.

When the plague returned, she was one of the few who ran toward the sick rather than away—caring for the dying, burying the dead, while others barricaded themselves in fear. She worked

tirelessly, never fell ill, and was credited in legends with miraculous cures.

Catherine was a mystic with what she called the gift of tears—a
soul so emotionally attuned that she wept for the pain of the
world.

I felt something stir in me when I read her story.

A resonance.

I needed to know more.

I began at the Church of San Domenico, a plain Gothic
structure where Catherine took Mass and began her mystical
journey. In a chapel there, frescoes depict scenes from her life—
and her head is preserved as a relic.

I then visited her family home, still standing on a quiet street
nearby. According to legend, she once fell into the fireplace
during an ecstatic trance, but emerged unharmed. Even as a
child, she prayed and spoke with God continuously.

From her home, I traced her steps up the marble staircase beside
the cathedral, following the path she walked each day to the
hospital of Santa Maria della Scala—now a museum. One of
Europe's oldest hospitals, it was founded in the 9th century as a
refuge for pilgrims and the poor.

Catherine came here daily as a volunteer nurse, filled with love and
tireless energy. She carried with her a lantern, a bottle of fragrant oil,
and a walking stick—all preserved now in a shrine. When her work
was done, she would retreat to a tiny chapel beneath the hospital,
next to the pit where the dead were buried. There, she prayed in a
small cell connected to the oratory, seeking solace and strength.

Walking those corridors, I felt an overwhelming heaviness. The walls held centuries of pain—so much death, so much grief. How had Catherine borne it all—tending to the sick and dying, day after day; burying the dead with her own hands. Even as her touch healed some, she could not heal all.

How did she carry the weight of being a healer whose patients die? How do any of us?

She once wrote:

> *"Suffering and sorrow increase in proportion to love."*

Catherine was a woman who loved deeply—and surely suffered deeply too. I had to pause to think about it. Loving others brings life the deepest meaning—but it also brings sorrow.

We cannot experience great love without suffering great grief as well.

@

Curious to find the small chapel where Catherine went to pray at night, we followed a narrow staircase beneath the hospital—but instead of a chapel, we stumbled into a labyrinth of old ruins. These were Roman foundations layered beneath the stones of the medieval hospital.

We wandered for what felt like hours, losing track of time and direction as we moved deeper into the underworld of Santa Maria della Scala.

And I realized: this is what my grief for my father had felt like. Buried deep beneath the structures of daily life. Hidden, silent, waiting.

We became completely lost, circling through the same passages, walking by the same artifacts over and over. But that too resembled the grief journey—there's no map.

The path is not linear. We are often disoriented.

Eventually, we stopped trying to outsmart the maze and simply chose one direction. We walked, one uncertain step at a time, until finally we emerged onto another level—where we found the chapel at last.

I n the past it had been the headquarters of a confraternity dedicated to caring for the sick and the dead—much like the Brotherhood of Death and Prayer we encountered in Monterosso.

This chapel, next to the hospital's burial pit, was named for the Archangel Michael, guide of souls to the underworld. Though women weren't permitted to join the confraternity, Catherine had been allowed to come there to pray. There's a small side cell where she would lie down to rest in the quiet hours of night. Today, that space holds a wooden statue of her reclining beneath a simple canopy.

I imagined her there—exhausted, heartbroken, seeking strength.

Did she ever wonder, as I did, if she had done enough?

Did she grieve the ones she could not save?

Did she question whether she was worthy of the calling she had embraced?

In that dim, cool chapel, I sat in a pew alone. It was a sanctuary of peace. And it was there—surrounded by the memory of Catherine's compassion—that I finally laid down my own burden.

The grief I had carried.

The guilt I hadn't dared to name.

This was the moment the previous five prayers had been preparing me for.

I wept.

I let the guilt surface—the guilt of not being able to save my father, or Julio. The guilt of not being enough that had hardened in silence, hidden in the ruins of my soul.

Here, in this sacred place where grief had been prayed over for centuries, I allowed myself to feel it fully.

Here, I said my Novena prayer:

"Please comfort Julio's family in their deep grief. Please honor the grief and the guilt I carry from caring for others who cannot be healed. Let this pain rise so it can be released."

Later, I would read these words from Catherine:

"It is only through shadows that one comes to know the light."

Shadow and light. *Chiaroscuro.* Wild and holy.

Here in Siena, on this descent into the soul's underworld, my grief became visible. And with it, the guilt that often accompanies loss. The archetypal guilt of a healer became—like a broken dream, an unfinished wall, an interrupted act of caring—a new vantage point for my life story.

.   .   .

A few years later, looking out from my own incomplete wall of sorrow, I could see more clearly:

Grief exists because of love.

And guilt too, strangely, is an expression of love.

In the light of grace, I saw that healer's guilt wears a halo of the best intentions: the greatest hope, the deepest human desire for life. As healers we devote ourselves to serving and preserving the vital spark of life—we train to be the best practitioners possible.

But Death—Sacred Death—is beyond our human control. Death has its own timing, its own perfection that is often hidden from our view. So we toil with our love, our hopes, our best intentions … and we lose everything we touch in the end.

It all dissolves away.

Guilt marks the space in time where we are in the darkness and cannot see the perfection of life and death.

And perhaps, like Siena's unfinished wall, it becomes our new vantage point—a symbol of what was interrupted but not abandoned; what was lost, but never unloved.

My guilt was slowly, agonizingly, being transformed over time into a deeper wisdom. I had been asked to be fully present to the suffering of the world and moreover to be present with my own suffering.

@

O n our last evening in Siena, we returned to Il Campo for dinner at an outdoor café. I had developed a fondness for this city that had plunged me back into darkness, but also held me gently—offering just enough light to reveal the hidden recesses of my grief.

Siena slowed me down so I could listen to the wisdom of my wounded heart and finally embrace the guilt that had haunted me for years.

We found a huge celebration taking place in the center of the square. Long tables were spread out for a festive dinner, with colorful banners and flags waving overhead, people cheering, music playing, and massive television screens set up to live-stream the entire event.

Our server told us this was a feast for the winners of the *Palio*—a horse race that has taken place twice a year in this very piazza for centuries.

Ten of the 17 *contrade* compete in a treacherous, fast-paced sprint around the oval while thousands of spectators pack every inch of space. The victorious *contrada* hosts a celebratory dinner in the weeks following the race—and that's what we had unknowingly stumbled upon.

To our surprise, as we watched, the winning horse was ushered in to thunderous applause and served his own dinner inside a special stall built among the tables.

Maroon and black linens bearing the image of an owl were visible on every table, and joyful participants wore bandanas and waved flags honoring their wise mascot. We learned that the motto of this *contrada* is "I see in the night," a reference to the owl's superpower—a trait that holds great significance on this life journey through times of darkness.

The celebration was especially exuberant because "The Contrada of the Noble Little Owl" (as they are named in Italian) hadn't won the Palio in 40 years. Not surprisingly, the entire city seemed to join in their triumph, and we were happy to be spectators of it all.

Never have I seen such a powerful display of enduring community—this ancient tradition, preserved since the Middle Ages, remains a vital heartbeat of the people and the place. That age-old ritual seemed to honor survival and persistence—not despite grief but because of it.

Even as the Duomo's unfinished wall tells of a ruined dream, the owl banners and this joyful feast—four decades in the making—remind us that life goes on.

Siena's grief is ancient, yes … but so is its joy.

Community creates the container that can safely hold both: sorrow and jubilation, the wild and the holy.

We feasted alongside the locals that night—on the periphery of their joy, but able to taste it, much like our Rosh Hashanah dinner in the Jewish Ghetto of Rome.

The server brought handmade *pici* pasta covered in wild boar ragù that had simmered for hours to develop the rich flavors and tender texture this regional specialty is known for.

Then we shared a slice of *panforte*—a dessert with ancient roots, born in Siena and once carried by crusaders to sustain them in their travels. Dense, chewy, and caramel-like, it was rich with honey and spices, studded with dried fruit and nuts, and dusted with powdered sugar.

Legend has it the original recipe, containing 17 ingredients to reflect the 17 *contrade* of Siena, was created by a nun in the

Middle Ages who infused the cake with medicinal spices to nourish the people during a siege.

To me, this "strong bread" was the perfect ending to our time in Siena—a city that cherishes ritual and tradition, much like grief itself: rich, complicated, and lasting.

I had discovered and traversed my inner darkness here, and I learned to see in the night, nourished like ancient pilgrims by the "old ways" that endure through time, offering safe shelter for sorrow and loss.

Crystal
In the darkness
deep beneath belief
and dogma and striving
I found what had been buried long ago,
marked as shame
reviled and rejected
left alone to harden into stone.
But in the presence of light …
this guilt sparkles
like crystal
in a hidden cave.
And now I hold gently
in my own two hands
this treasure
of misguided love.

NOVENA DAY 7

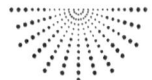

CORTONA - CHURCH OF ST. MARGARET

There is often a feeling of shame attached to the survivors of suicide, a hidden doubt that they might not have done enough to prevent this death. This is a doubling of the pain.

— FRANCIS WELLER

W e left the reddish-brown bricks of Siena in a rental car headed toward Cortona—the village made famous by the book (and film) *Under the Tuscan Sun*. I knew it would be crowded with tourists, but I was drawn by the chance to stay at a family-owned olive orchard and glimpse an entirely different way of life.

As we drove through the winding roads and hills of Tuscany, I had time to contemplate the experiences of the past several days:

In Monterosso, among lemon trees and wild salt air, I tasted joy again. I let the sunlight touch my face. I thought I had broken through—that grief had released me. But grief has its own map, and it does not follow the paths we would choose.

In Siena, the descent came—swift, unexpected, undeniable. Guilt rose from the dark corners where I had hidden it. But perhaps the beauty and joy of the Ligurian coast had made me stronger, strong enough to withstand the fall into the darkness.

I understand that this is the way of all true pilgrimages: the Hero's Journey, the Dark Night of the Soul, the wild spiral of healing.

We rise. We fall. We rise again.

Grief is not a flat, linear path. It winds and curves like a river, circling through loss and light, through falling apart and weaving together.

And when guilt attaches itself to grief, it tangles and complicates the journey even further. If grace finds us on this path, it does not lift us out of the pain—but it holds us as we fall deeper into it.

That's what I learned in Siena: to allow the river of grief to take its course and follow the flow wherever it leads.

A rriving at our stop we found an old olive orchard and mill with a two-story farmhouse made of brown sandstone and clay. Our lodging was next door in a smaller stone building that had been beautifully refurbished inside.

The farm was situated on a terrace below the hilltop town of Cortona—a five-mile drive by car or a one-mile walk on dirt paths up the hill. Rows of cypress trees lined the road in the distance, tiered groves of gray-green olive trees spread outside our back window, and wildflowers were scattered throughout the yard—including one with tiny pink blossoms that danced in the wind, nicknamed the "whirling butterfly." Its delicate petals reaching toward the sun reminded me each time I saw it that transformation can also arrive with the slightest whisper.

The small kitchen in our lodge was equipped with a Moka espresso maker and a basket of fruit from the orchard. Our hosts had also left a loaf of fresh wholegrain bread, a flask of greenish-gold olive oil pressed in their mill, and a jar of homemade granola for our breakfast.

We felt at home in this special place, once again connected to the stillness and beauty of nature—a fitting hostel for this pilgrimage of mourning.

Life is good, indeed, when measured in these small moments of grace and light. "Gratitude for Life"—a memory from the Grazie Bridge in Florence—was present that day.

During a tour of the olive orchard, we learned that in Italy, olive oil is far more than just an ingredient for cooking. Historically, it has been used as fuel for lamps, as medicine and healing balm, in cosmetics and soaps, to anoint kings and priests in sacred ceremonies, and to bless the sick and dying. Since ancient times, it has been called "liquid gold," a substance of profound value at every family table.

These family farmers tend their small groves with almost religious devotion—refusing to use "modern" harvesting methods that might harm the trees or bruise the olives. They understand the impact of even the subtlest shifts in soil, sunlight, wind, and moisture, and know how to adapt to whatever Nature offers—or withholds—each season. They also know exactly when the olives are ready to be harvested.

We saw shelves lined with bottles of the precious greenish-gold liquid, and we witnessed how the olives, once retrieved, are carefully washed and cleaned before being pressed to release their oil. These family farms produce just enough olive oil each year for their own use, occasionally selling or bartering any surplus.

But the harvest is more than an act of physical survival—it is a sacred ritual, a connection to Nature and its rhythms, to history and ancestors, to culture, meaning, and purpose.

It is a foundation of emotional and spiritual well-being.

To step into this ecosystem of growth, sustainability, nurturing, harvesting—and even grieving the death of a tree—was beneficial for the mourning and healing journey I was undertaking.

Cortona is a hilltop town that dates all the way back to the mysterious Etruscan civilization, which flourished long before the rise of Rome. With its medieval architecture and winding streets, Cortona feels charming and intimate. Its small size offered a welcome relief after the extensive walking required to navigate Siena.

On our first visit we saw older townspeople reading newspapers on the steps of the city hall and sipping espresso in metal chairs outside the café—a peaceful morning haven.

Life feels slow here—suspended in time perhaps.

At the Etruscan Museum we learned what little is known about the Etruscan civilization that flourished in what is now Tuscany from approximately the 8th century BCE to the 1st.

One exhibit featured a "mourning slab"—a funeral bed carved from tufa stone, found in a tomb. The stone was etched with the figures of eight women, each in a different posture of mourning —tearing their hair, covering their faces.

Much of what archaeologists have learned about the Etruscans has come from their tombs. We know that they grieved and honored their dead just as we do. But from this slab and from other burial displays we would later see in Paestum, it became clear that mourning practices were not just expressions of grief— they were tools for healing.

In some ancient societies professional mourners were hired to wail and tear their hair, helping loved ones move through the shock and numbness of loss. These rituals were designed to unlock the body and heart.

I understood the need for that assistance—I had been suspended in my own grief for far too long.

It struck me that much of our historical knowledge about ancient civilizations comes to us through their dead—tombs, mausoleums, and sarcophagi etched with stories of life and the agony of loss. Even a Neanderthal archeological site in France revealed evidence of an intentional burial. Death has always been sacred.

The grief I carried often made me feel alienated from the people around me—coworkers and friends who didn't understand why it hadn't "gone away" yet. But grief is not a failure.

Every person who mourns enters a brotherhood of sorrow with all who have known this pain across time. It is a vast fellowship. And we hold one another with care during painful seasons.

· · ·

Our next stop was the Diocesan Museum where we viewed a Roman sarcophagus—again, society telling its story through the dead—and some Renaissance paintings. There we saw a breathtaking work by local artist Luca Signorelli called *The Mourning of Christ* from 1502.

It is said that Signorelli used the body of his own son—who had died from the plague—as the model for Christ's perfect anatomy.

Grief is palpable on the faces of the mourners: shock, numbness, sorrow, overwhelm, anger. Signorelli knew the face of sorrow. He used the paintbrush to express his exquisite pain—and to make grief visible for the rest of us.

Art reminds us that we are never the first to feel what we feel —and we will not be the last.

In every brushstroke, every carved line, every sculpted branch — grief lives on ... to help us remember:

We are part of a larger human story.

To be human is to love and to lose. Grief is not a flaw but a thread that connects us to one another. Across centuries, continents, and civilizations.

We are never alone in our mourning.

Our sorrow echoes back to the very beginning of time.

In our explorations around the village, we learned that St. Margaret was the patron saint of Cortona and that a church had been dedicated to her on a hillside just outside of town. It is a well-known pilgrimage site in Italy for Catholics who follow St.

Francis, and I knew intuitively that I needed to see it—and to offer my next Novena prayer there.

We followed the pilgrims' route to the church, up a steep hill on a stone path where, apparently, devoted pilgrims sometimes walk on their knees all the way to the top. For me, it was a meditative walk.

As I prepared for the Novena prayer, I tried to contemplate my grief—but the emotion that kept rising was guilt.

Once again, I was flooded with self-recriminating thoughts: my failure to save my patient, my failure to save my father—just as I had experienced in Siena. Feelings of shame and unworthiness haunted me as I plodded up the path, troubled by the resurgence of these old wounds.

Why now? Why here?

When I reached the church, I paused to read about the life of the beloved Saint Margaret, and it quickly became clear why all of these turbulent emotions were surfacing—and why this was the perfect place for the seventh prayer.

Margaret had endured a lifetime of pain and suffering before she dedicated her life to service. Her mother died when she was just seven years old, leaving her childhood marked by grief and a loss of safety. She entered an abusive marriage at a young age, then met her true love and became his mistress—an arrangement that led to shame and societal rejection.

When her lover died traumatically, Margaret was plunged into unbearable grief, which eventually led her to the teachings of St. Francis. She vowed to dedicate her life to caring for the poor, the sick, and the needy.

Like Catherine of Siena, she never became a nun, but she took a vow of poverty and lived the rest of her life in penitence, always struggling with feelings of guilt and shame.

M argaret's story resonated deeply with me. I allowed myself to be swept away by my own buried emotions— emotions that I had repressed since my father's death and from much earlier in my life. Julio's death had "taken the lid off," and I could no longer contain what had been hidden.

But I was in the right place: where Margaret had also wrestled with shame and unworthiness, where she had sought a sense of worth after the shame of having a relationship with a married man.

I hadn't recognized it until that very moment but deeper still beneath the guilt I carried for my father's death was the earlier shame of my own affair with my current husband—who was married to someone else at that time—so many years in the past. No wonder I was drawn to this church for the Novena prayer.

Guilt resides deep in the darkness of the heart, no matter the source. But now everything I had repressed for so long was rising to the surface. And I was connected through all of it to this saint I had never heard of before.

T he church brochure said that after Margaret's death, rumors began to spread that her lifeless body had healing powers. Pilgrims visited her grave and reported miraculous cures from this humble, hard-working saint.

Eventually, the current basilica was constructed to accommodate the many visitors coming to ask for healing. When Margaret's body was moved into the new church, they found that it had not decomposed at all—a sign often cited in the path to sainthood.

Her relics now rest in a glass case near the altar. I watched as dozens of pilgrims entered the church, filed past her body, whispered prayers, and lit candles.

I joined the procession and slowly made my way forward, thinking about Margaret's lifetime of guilt and shame that led to her sainthood—as opposed to Catherine's path of purity and devotion, which also led to sainthood.

Margaret and Catherine—two different journeys, wild and holy —both touched by grace. Both women found their purpose as healers.

When I reached the glass case that held Margaret's remains, I spontaneously reached out, as if to touch her.

I felt a spark of love and acceptance—like the moment I beheld Mary's face in the *Pietà*. I was safe here. I was still seen and held by the Divine Feminine, who carries our grief—and all of our guilt—along with us on our journeys.

Lighting a votive candle, I paused to pray:

"Please help Julio's family carry the grief they've been asked to bear. Please help me carry my own guilt and shame and transform them into blessings in my life. May I have the courage to find the path to my true purpose."

There are many roads that can lead us to our purpose. There is no right or wrong journey, no better or worse person, no true success or failure in our efforts to do good in the world.

We each take what life gives us and do the best we can to make something beautiful from it.

I wondered if Margaret ever found relief from her guilt while she was alive. I hoped that she had—that she felt the sweet taste of forgiveness on her tongue, the soothing waters of compassion on her skin.

At the time, I couldn't see it—but now I understand that all the reasons I had never been able to talk about my father's suicide rose to the surface on the pilgrim's road to St. Margaret's Basilica.

The guilt and shame, the stigma of suicide, the fear of judgment, the lack of answers to so many questions—a pain so overwhelming I had relegated it to the depths of my vast heart. There it had been stored for decades—unembraced and unhealed—while it secretly wreaked havoc on my health.

Cortona was the beginning of another long journey: unearthing what I had not been able to face. Truly what was released there was the guilt of simply being human—imperfect in a flawed world.

When we returned to the stillness of the little orchard where we were staying, I felt drawn to take my shoes off and walk barefoot through the garden—between rosemary and lavender, past wild daisies and poppies swaying in the breeze.

Smooth stone steps led past terracotta pots overflowing with geraniums to a wooden bench beside a small stream. I placed my feet in the rippling water and let it wash away the dust of the ancient path of grief I had been walking.

Something was beginning to shift inside me once again—and this time, it felt powerful and deeper than ever before.

I still wasn't sure how I could carry all that had been buried in the Shadow. But as I dried my feet with my sweater and anointed them with olive oil lotion in that garden, I sensed that what was wild inside of me was slowly becoming holy.

And it was good.

I t was beginning to dawn on me that this trip I had planned a year earlier was, somehow, exactly the pilgrimage I needed in this moment—to navigate my sorrow over Julio's death, and to unlock the complicated grief I still carried for Dad and for my past history.

Each day, I seemed to be in the right place at the right time. There were little signs and symbols everywhere—especially when I wasn't expecting them.

We wandered around the village on our last evening until it was time for our cooking class to begin—a highlight of our stay in Cortona.

On one narrow side street, with houses overhanging above, I saw a sign for the Circle of Life Gallery and followed my curiosity inside. There, I stepped into a modern, luminous space filled with glass and concrete structures showcasing the exquisite, evocative sculptures of artist Andrea Roggi.

His designs were breathtaking: olive trees made of distressed and bent bronze fragments that formed the most fragile and delicate leaves and branches imaginable. The trunks were composed of intertwined human forms—bodies reaching upward, their arms merging with the branches above. Their legs seemed to dissolve into the earth, becoming deep, sturdy roots below.

Later, I learned that Roggi uses lost wax casting, an ancient technique once practiced by the Etruscans. A mold is formed around a wax sculpture, which is then melted and poured away—lost—leaving a hollow space to receive molten bronze.

That image has stayed with me. It mirrors the journey of grief, and of spiritual growth. Often, we are melted inside by the pain we encounter—hollowed out so that something new might take shape. And what emerges from this process is sacred—beautiful in its fragility, like Roggi's sculptures.

I was reminded of the Apollo and Daphne statue in Rome, which had also moved me so deeply—capturing the instant of transformation, the breath held in the threshold between two states.

I had whispered, with tears in my eyes, "This looks like love... like the moment when love becomes life."

We receive our lives from the earth, and we give them back again through our bodies as we die.

O n one of our tours through an ancient olive grove, we were shown trees nearly 1,000 years old—trees that had lived through the Black Death, the Renaissance, the World Wars, and still stood in the sun-dappled silence of the present.

We learned that as olive trees age, their trunks grow massive and gnarled, but outer layers begin to die and fall away. Meanwhile, the roots below push up a new trunk from the ground, a few feet away, which eventually merges with the upper branches of the original tree.

Over time, the new growth replaces the old, while remaining connected to it. These trees, we were told, appear to be walking. There is always something new emerging to nourish what is still alive—life carrying on even as parts of the whole die.

. . .

T hose walking trees became, for me, a powerful reminder of
      how we carry our grief—and how we carry our dead—
with us. We continue walking forward, creating new aspects of
life, yet we are never alone.

Our dead are with us always, shaping who we become.

When I saw Roggi's bronze sculptures of olive trees, my mind
immediately flashed back to those ancient walking trees. I saw
the pain of loss, but also the beauty of continuity—life finding a
way to blossom and bloom again, feeding us, nourishing us,
supporting us.

Whatever has died remains a part of us. And we become our
greatest, most fully human selves not by discarding it—but by
embracing it all. Embracing the losses, carrying the pain,
honoring the grief, and even holding the guilt and the failures.
That is how we grow into our most courageous and compassionate selves.

R oggi's Tree of Life sculptures embody rootedness and
      transcendence at once—a visible expression of the path I
had been walking.

His website reads: "Part of us is on the ground, but most of us is
above the sky."

We are always navigating two journeys: one grounded in the
archaeology of our grief, the other reaching toward the
cosmology of the stars.

I cherished this metaphor of trees that live alongside what has
died—integrating the past, not abandoning it. Turning love into
life, like Roggi's sculptures.

These little moments of synchronicity were beginning to speak to me.

◎

For our last evening at the olive orchard, we had a cooking class with a local cook named Chicca. She told us that in Italy, cooking is a family experience—filled with unique recipes that have been handed down for generations.

The key is to use fresh ingredients that are locally grown and in season. Italian cooking is often slow, built on simple techniques, but every dish is handmade and rich with love, care, and tradition.

I was assigned to make gnocchi, which was a first for me. Chicca's family recipe didn't include potatoes as some do. Instead, I mixed together semolina flour, milk, butter, egg yolks, Parmesan, and a dash of nutmeg.

We shaped the dough into small balls using an ice cream scoop, placed them on a baking sheet with butter, sage, and more Parmesan on top, and baked them for 20 minutes. I had never made anything with my own two hands that tasted so delicious.

Other members of our group made puttanesca sauce with olives, capers, garlic, olive oil, and fresh tomato. Served over handmade pasta, it was pungent and flavorful.

Chicca told us that "puttanesca" meant prostitute, but didn't explain how the sauce got its name. By then, we were too busy eating to ask.

The meal also featured spinach lasagna, baked fennel, green

beans with tomatoes, and a peppery arugula salad—an abundant Italian feast.

There was laughter in all corners of the kitchen that evening as we sat around large wooden tables, sharing travel stories like old friends.

We feasted together for hours—this meal cooked communally with total strangers who, somehow, felt closer than family by the end of the night.

The little village of Cortona—barely noticed by those who flock to Rome and Florence—had become an ideal site for my pilgrimage.

It had offered me ancient grief and mourning practices, art that holds space for sorrow while reaching toward transcendence, olive trees that nourish and survive tragedy, and a wounded saint who carried her guilt and became a healer for all of us imperfect ones.

There was a shifting... a loosening of the tight grip guilt had on my heart. The Novenas were changing everything.

And joy was sneaking in through the cracks in my ruined trip to Italy.

@

Intertwined
Grief and Love
intertwined
cradling both life and death
in arms that reach
forever to the sky
and root deep into the earth.
There is no room
for guilt or shame
in these branches
dissolving into
stardust and ash
that which has always been
born of Love.

NOVENA DAY 8

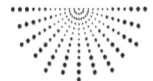

ASSISI - CHURCH OF ST. MARY OF THE ANGELS

Forgive yourself. The supreme act of forgiveness is when you forgive yourself for all the wounds you've created in your life. Forgiveness is an act of self-love.

— MIGUEL ANGEL RUIZ MACIAS

The next stop on our journey was the city of Assisi, which I had looked forward to visiting from the moment I began planning this trip a year earlier. I'd been a fan of St. Francis since childhood—even though I wasn't Catholic—because his story and teachings had always appealed to me.

Born into a wealthy family, Francis had a reputation in his youth for partying and revelry. Seeking to be a hero, he joined the war against the neighboring city of Perugia, where he was captured in battle and imprisoned for a year.

That long confinement left him changed—disillusioned with violence and war, and yearning for deeper meaning.

One pivotal story from his life tells how Francis was riding outside Assisi when he encountered a leper by the roadside. All his life, he had been repulsed by the sight and smell of leprosy—a disease that carried deep stigma and fear.

Like most people at the time, he would have gone out of his way to avoid a leper. But on that particular day, something shifted. Francis felt an inner call to approach the man despite his revulsion.

Overcoming his fear, he embraced the man and offered him a kiss—an act that symbolized facing everything within himself that he had long rejected and cast into shadow.

In that surrender, Francis experienced a profound awakening. He couldn't heal the man or change his illness, but in healing his own woundedness, he discovered the deep compassion that would define his life and teachings.

He had found God in that encounter—and the power of love.

Soon after, Francis publicly renounced his family's wealth—including his fine clothing—and devoted his life to God. He preached peace and love for all living beings, restored crumbling churches, and lived in voluntary poverty.

He saw nature as a reflection of God's beauty and goodness, and his joy and humility drew followers into a new way of worship.

His first recorded miracle took place in the village of Gubbio, where he tamed a vicious wolf with only his words—an event commemorated by the statue we saw in Monterosso al Mare near the cemetery.

Francis wandered the hills of Tuscany, preaching his gospel of joy outdoors in the local language rather than in the grand Latin of the church.

Today, he remains one of the most beloved saints in all of Christendom. His teachings resonate far beyond religion—integrating the feminine wisdom of connectedness, intuition, harmony, and soul with the masculine ideals of action, intellect, form, and differentiation.

His message is one of wholeness.

As a child, I was especially drawn to the story of Francis's sermon to the birds. According to the legend, he once approached a flock of birds and spoke to them about being grateful for their blessings. The birds, it's said, listened with rapt attention, never taking their eyes off him. I loved that story—because I, too, had a tender love for small birds.

Every winter, tiny sparrows would nest in the corner of the metal awning above my bedroom window. Each night before bed, I'd peek out to check on them, whisper goodnight, and wish for their warmth and safety.

Somehow, I felt sure that Francis would understand. He would have approved of my concern for those tiny feathered beings.

So long before this trip became a Novena journey, visiting the hometown of St. Francis had been at the top of my travel list. And once the grief pilgrimage began in Rome—though I didn't yet know how or where each of the Novena prayers would unfold—I decided that I wanted to say one at the Basilica of St. Francis in Assisi.

Looking back, I now recognize another reason I was always drawn to St. Francis: he reminded me of my father.

Dad was a quiet, humble man of deep integrity and unwavering loyalty. He had a profound connection to nature and took me on countless outdoor adventures—camping, hiking, fishing, hunting, exploring.

He taught me how to spot animals in the wild, recognize their tracks, identify bird songs, and find constellations in the night sky. He would point to a vast prairie of wheatgrass rippling in the wind and say, "This is where God lives."

He cared little for material things and frequently gave what he had to those in need. Though he was a man of few words, he could be a masterful storyteller and humorist when he chose to be.

After his death, we learned the full scope of his quiet generosity. He had worked at his family's gas station since he was fourteen and had helped countless people who came through in hardship —repairing their cars for free, filling their gas tanks, handing them bags of groceries from the market down the street.

When his obituary ran in the local paper, scores of people came to the station to tell us their stories. Some said they had been able to survive—and eventually thrive—because of my father's help.

He never spoke of it. He never asked for recognition. To me, he was a saint—a modern-day Francis in coveralls.

No wonder I was shattered by his death.

All I ever wanted was to be someone as kind and good as my dad. That his life ended so suddenly and violently was incomprehensible to me.

How could someone with so much love in his heart find it impossible to stay alive in this world? And why hadn't I—who tried so hard to walk in his footsteps—been able to help him?

There had never been time to honor my father for the difference he made. Shame and guilt consumed every moment after his

suicide. So this Novena prayer in Assisi felt like the most important ritual of the entire pilgrimage. A chance to honor St. Francis
—and also my dad.

And I was determined to make it happen.

We arrived in Assisi by bus and were able to see the city
from miles away as we approached. In contrast to the
reddish-brown bricks of Siena and the yellow-tan stones of
Cortona, Assisi—built from pink and white limestone quarried
from Mount Subasio—gleams in the sunlight with a sacred
glow.

The sight was breathtaking. I knew this visit would be the highlight of our entire trip.

The parking lot where we disembarked was completely filled
with enormous tour and charter buses, row after row, with
crowds of people streaming from every direction.

We didn't need to search for the path uphill to the city—we were
swept along by the tide of pilgrims headed the same way. This
was surprising. We hadn't encountered anything close to these
numbers in any other city on our journey.

Dragging our suitcases up the long hill, slightly dazed, we tried to
get our bearings. We decided to find our hotel, which took us
through the throngs of people—many of them wearing clerical
robes from various religions, sects, and countries—and up and
down steep streets and staircases.

"What is going on here?" we asked the man at the front desk once
we finally located our tiny hotel.

"Oh!" he replied with joy and pride, "It is the Feast Day of St.

Francis! People have come from all over the world to celebrate together!"

Oh my goodness. How had we planned a random one-day visit to Assisi months ago and managed to arrive on this one sacred day of the year—when the rest of the world was also here?

What bad timing, I thought.

But the hotel owner was kind and warm as he welcomed us. He showed us a tiny rooftop deck above an attic that served as the "visitor's lounge," stocked with snacks and beverages available to us all day at no charge.

In our room, he offered us a complimentary guided audio tour of Assisi, complete with headphones and a map. His generosity and care were a balm after the overwhelming arrival.

We tried the audio tour, but it was difficult to focus amidst the masses of people everywhere we went. And more disturbing to me were the small tables and kiosks lining nearly every street and square, selling all manner of Francis-themed souvenirs—everything from bobblehead dolls to high-end Nativity scenes, from mugs and umbrellas to sandals and snack trays.

I magining myself in Francis's place, beholding this commercialism in his beloved, sacred city, I felt a wave of dismay. How had his message of simplicity and poverty been so blatantly exploited for profit? I was baffled. And deeply disappointed.

Still, I wanted to fulfill my goal of saying the Novena prayer inside the Basilica. I held onto hope that it would be peaceful and sacred there. We made our way slowly in that direction—but as we neared the church, it became clear we wouldn't even get close.

The courtyard and surrounding plaza were packed with people. A major event was taking place inside, and the crowd was pushing to get in. This was clearly not the moment for a contemplative visit.

We decided to regroup and return to the Basilica later in the evening, once the crowds had dispersed.

Thankfully, our guidebook reminded us to take the backstreets— and to look up. As we made our way back to the hotel, we noticed that nearly every doorway, balcony, and window was adorned with hanging gardens of geraniums, petunias, impatiens, and lobelia.

Apparently, Assisi holds a flower competition every June, and the results linger long afterward. The city was blooming—literally— with beauty and joy.

I read that even in Francis's day, Assisi could become crowded and congested, and that he often sought refuge at a hermitage on the slopes of Mount Subasio for solitude and peace.

Still determined to say the eighth Novena prayer in the Basilica later in the day, we decided to first take a spontaneous hike to the hermitage—just as Francis himself might have done.

We didn't have a map to the hermitage, but we followed the signs as we trudged uphill along a narrow paved road with no shoulder. Already, I felt more relaxed just being away from the hustle and noise of the city.

Soon we found a footpath that veered off the road into the woods —one of the ancient trails Francis himself might have walked. It led us into a forest near the hermitage, where we eventually came upon a rustic garden and an old stone altar covered with handmade crosses of all sizes, crafted from twigs and branches.

In a nearby grotto we discovered bronze sculptures of three monks, and just beyond them, the caves where Francis's companions—Brother Rufino and Brother Masseo—would go to pray.

A t last, this place felt like a proper home for the St. Francis I so admired: simple structures set within the quiet beauty of nature, surrounded by all that was wild and holy.

Inside the friary, we were shown the small cave where Francis once retreated in prayer, now cradled within a monastery built around it. In the courtyard still stands the tree where he is said to have preached to the birds.

The solitude and natural beauty of this place were calming and reassuring to me, and I was grateful we had made the trek. It felt right that Francis would have chosen this sacred grove to commune with the nature he so loved and glorified in his Canticle of the Sun—praising the sun and fire as his brothers, and the moon and water as his sisters.

And in recognition of the Cycle of Life his canticle even included a verse honoring Sister Death, which he composed the day before he died.

F rancis's reverence for nature was actually world-changing, according to art historians. Before Francis, the Church had taught that all things of this world were evil—including nature herself. Only God was sacred.

Medieval art reflected this belief: religious figures were depicted in flat, two-dimensional space with expressionless faces and no background—no trees, animals, or other signs of the natural world.

In contrast, Renaissance painting—just a century or so later—was radically different: perspective, lifelike forms, landscapes, and emotional expression transformed sacred art into something more fully human and alive.

Francis, it seems, sparked a cultural and spiritual revolution—one that bridged the gap between Medieval austerity and Renaissance humanism—by teaching that the natural world was a gift from God, and not only good, but a manifestation of God Himself.

According to Francis, we were meant to live in harmony with nature, not dominate or control it. And the power of his message —so widely embraced in his lifetime and beyond, as evidenced by the massive crowds we encountered in Assisi—was enough to influence culture over time, even shaping the way nature came to be depicted in art.

The Italian painter Giotto, a devoted follower of St. Francis, is considered the first naturalist artist in Europe. Living and working during that transitional era, Giotto helped usher in the Renaissance through his radical new approach.

His frescoes in the Basilica—depicting scenes from Francis's life with landscapes, trees, and real people showing emotion—were revolutionary for their time.

This was one reason I was so determined to visit the Basilica and say the Novena prayer there.

It would be perfect.

At least, according to my plans.

©

From the peace of the hermitage and surrounding forest, we walked back to Assisi—thankfully downhill all the way—and into the chaotic mix of pilgrims, clerics, and tourists, all trying to experience a sacred moment on this Feast Day of St. Francis. Unfortunately we soon learned that both the Upper and Lower Basilicas would remain closed to tourists for the rest of the day.

How could this be?

I was crushed—and angry. Angry at myself for not checking the calendar more carefully in my planning. Angry at the entire Catholic Church for not accommodating my plans. For a moment I spiraled into negativity, believing the 8th Novena prayer was ruined because I couldn't fulfill the climactic highlight I had imagined.

But slowly, I came to my senses.

Of course there are other churches. Of course I can still say a prayer. I would simply have to make the best of things and find another place.

I realized I had to surrender my plans in that moment—there was no way around it.

Looking back, I can see how precarious a spiritual journey can be —fraught with false hopes and expectations that become traps and deep pitfalls along the way.

Facing disappointment and loss is a rough way to get acquainted with the futile escapades of the ego, but necessary if we are ever to become our genuine, authentic selves.

Surrender is hard.

Loving yourself through the act of surrender is harder still.

. . .

One small paragraph in the guidebook caught my eye. It described the Porziuncola, a small old chapel on the outskirts of Assisi that had been given to Francis when he was first starting his order. It was abandoned and in disrepair when he received it, but Francis lovingly restored the forgotten building, where legend says the singing of angels could sometimes be heard.

Historians note that it was here, in this humble chapel, that Francis began to understand his calling to care for the poor, where he faced temptations and had visions, and where he welcomed the young woman who would become Saint Clare into the community.

When Francis sensed his death approaching, he asked to be brought back to this very place—the site where his work had begun.

A tiny chapel in the woods.

I recognized this would be the perfect place for the prayer— not a grand, vast Basilica surrounded by souvenir stalls, but a simple, unassuming chapel where Francis practiced his faith.

The little church is now encased within the massive Basilica of Saint Mary of the Angels, built around it to protect it. But the original structure remains intact, and I was able to go inside and spend a quiet moment there.

Rough square stones are still visible within the chapel—the very stones placed by Francis's own hands when he first repaired it.

Above the altar is a fresco depicting the moment Mary receives the news from the angel Gabriel that she will bear the son of

God. Her face shows surprise and even a trace of doubt as she struggles to accept her calling.

She has been asked to carry the full circle of life—to hold in her arms both the newborn Christ and, ultimately, his dead body—for the sake of the world. That's a harsh request, demanding surrender and acceptance without resentment.

For me, at that time in my journey, I had only just unearthed the massive specter of guilt I'd been carrying—exposed in Cortona—and I was now struggling with it daily. I had repressed that guilt for years, but now it was uncovered and raw.

The disappointment and self-recrimination I experienced over my plans for Assisi being "ruined" were rooted in that same wound. I hadn't yet learned how to tend it.

As I stood before the little altar in the chapel, I didn't know what I needed or exactly what to ask for.

But the beauty of grace is that it finds us where we are and brings what we need—even when we can't name it.

I arrived in the chapel by grace. That much is clear to me now.

Without clarity or certainty, I returned to my simple prayer for Julio's family:

"May they find peace within their grief.

And may I be shown what I need next."

I understood that I had to learn how to surrender, how to stop trying to control everything, but I didn't know how to do that. That was the answer I longed for, though I doubted I would receive it.

. . .

After a few more moments in the chapel, I stepped out to visit the Chapel of the Transit, built over the old infirmary cell where Francis had actually died.

In a biography of Francis by St. Bonaventure, I read that at the moment of his death, a flock of larks flew over the cell "whirling around for a long time with unusual joy"—saying goodbye to an old friend.

And suddenly, a poignant memory surfaced.

A meadowlark had once landed beside me while I wept at my father's grave, the day after his funeral. That little bird stayed the entire time I was there, singing its haunting song over and over again—the very song my father had taught me to recognize on our hikes when I was a child.

Then in the brochure I'd been given about the Porziuncola, I read that Francis had requested a special blessing: that all who entered the chapel with a repentant heart would receive forgiveness.

And there it was.

Francis had given me an answer to my Novena prayer long before I even knew what to ask for. Forgiveness—for myself. For my failures and my unknowing. For not being able to stop what happened. For not saving my father. For not saving Julio. But also for just being human—woven through with flaws and imperfections.

The grace of self-forgiveness—embracing my own shunned and exiled parts—was what I most needed. It was the balm that could soften the guilt I carried—the guilt that had entangled my grief and kept it from flowing, from transforming.

That forgiveness had already been granted—by Francis who sanctified the chapel for visitors—and by my father in the song of the meadowlark at his graveside.

But it would take years of work to allow it into my life, to let it soften the edges of my heart, and gentle the wild beast within.

And yet...

This was a beginning.

I ronically, once I let go of my insistence on doing the 8th Novena prayer in the Basilica of St. Francis, the doors finally opened and I was able to go inside. The church is truly breath-taking—not with the ornate grandeur of St. Peter's in Rome, but with its simple and contemplative atmosphere.

A fitting tribute to the humble saint of joy.

I later learned that this church was built in just 25 years, a remarkable achievement for the 13th century.

In comparison, Santa Maria del Fiore in Florence took 140 years to complete, while the construction of the Duomo in Siena—with its famously unfinished wall—spanned 165 years.

The Basilica's swift construction was a testament to the immense popularity of the beloved saint and the desire to create a shrine that could house his relics and welcome pilgrims from around the world—even though St. Francis himself never sought the fame and devotion he continues to inspire today.

W e entered through the Lower Basilica where the walls are adorned with frescoes depicting parallel scenes from the lives of Christ and Francis, connected by a ceiling of stars. I was mesmerized by those stars—gold against a background of deep blue—which created a sense of being held by the Universe: intimacy within infinity, a mirror within the unknown.

I think Francis would be pleased by that. His "precious and beautiful" stars—as he called them in his Canticle of the Sun—have their place overseeing the stories of his brief life of pure love.

In the transept of the lower church, there is an example of the revolutionary art of Giotto, Europe's first naturalist painter, who —as I mentioned earlier—was inspired by the teachings of Francis.

His depiction of the Crucifixion shows angels and humans alike expressing raw grief and despair, with Mary having fainted in anguish. This naturalistic portrayal was a radical step toward the humanism of Renaissance art, which would flourish a half-century later.

The Upper Basilica is equally spectacular, featuring stained glass windows from the 13th and 14th centuries—among the oldest in Italy.

The frescoed walls—again by Giotto and his assistants—depict 28 scenes from the life of St. Francis: renouncing his possessions, creating the first nativity scene, his visions and miracles, and— my favorite—preaching to the birds, supposedly beneath the tree we had seen at the hermitage. The birds are of many different species, representing the diversity of life, all beloved and protected by the Creator.

These frescoes were designed to speak directly to the countless pilgrims who would visit this shrine over the centuries with this message: you, like the birds and all of nature, are cherished by a loving God. Again, these works of art—so earthy and tender— planted the seeds that would blossom fully in the Renaissance.

Near the front entrance, we looked up to see tan patches on the ceiling where frescoes had been shattered by an earthquake in 1997. Two monks and two art scholars who were standing below were killed by the falling fragments.

A reminder that nothing in this world is exempt from impermanence—not even the holiest of places.

Nothing material can outlast death.

As dusk approached, we wandered down Via San Francesco and took in the sights of Assisi once again, appreciating the beauty of the city with new eyes. I imagined St. Francis himself walking these cobblestones, greeting the people, the birds, and the dogs and cats, too.

On the eastern edge of town, we found ourselves standing before another church: the Basilica of Saint Clare. I knew little about Clare except that she had given up her noble status at just eighteen to follow Francis. He had welcomed her to the community on Palm Sunday and cut her hair in the Porziuncola.

But I soon learned that Clare was a close friend and soul companion of Francis. Both were powerfully called to their paths —he to travel and minister to large crowds, she to stay cloistered with her sisters, the Poor Clares, for all of her life.

Clare embraced a life of poverty, service, and devotion, despite suffering greatly from physical ailments that left her bedridden for much of her adulthood. She believed that love shapes who we are and should be expressed through service to others.

Clare and her sisters anchored the Franciscan movement in Assisi, while Francis and his brothers carried the message far and wide. The sisters welcomed the brothers when they returned, eager to hear Francis' stories—told with laughter, singing, and joy.

But Francis died at the age of 44, leaving Clare bereft. She had helped care for him in his final illness but wasn't at his bedside at the end. When Francis was told that Clare was weeping in sorrow, he sent a final message to her, promising that she and the sisters would see him again.

Clare lived for 27 more years without her dear Francis. She carried on his teachings, keeping his vision alive through her devotion. Her ongoing love for him fueled her work and comforted her grieving heart.

Theirs was a love story—not of traditional romance, but of deep spiritual connection and shared calling.

I read that Clare's church was built intentionally on the opposite end of Assisi from that of St. Francis. The two serene structures face each other so that Clare and Francis, soul companions in life, could remain turned toward one another even in death—holding the village they loved in the embrace of their memory.

I stood between those mirrored cathedrals, just as I had stood between the two churches in Monterosso al Mare, reminded to hold both life and death in my awareness. But this time, *I* was being held—in the cradled arms of two saints: Divine masculine and Sacred feminine, wild and holy, light and dark.

Their message to me was of the transformative power of love, and the grace of forgiveness that is bestowed before it is even sought.

In the end, the visit to Assisi had not gone according to plan. I had to surrender my itinerary—reluctantly at first—in order to receive the experiences that were waiting for me there. Again, this is the essence of pilgrimage, especially a pilgrimage of grief.

We do not know for certain where we are going, or how things will work out. But it is the willingness to take the first step into the unknown that changes everything.

Grace will rise to meet us where we are, and help us find our destination when the time is right.

That night we found a café that spilled down a steep staircase near our hotel. Seated on a small platform jutting from one of the steps, we were in our own little world—feasting and celebrating a day of twists and turns, emotional ups and downs, shadows and light.

I ordered *Zuppa di farro*—a hearty soup made with beans, chewy farro grains, pancetta, vegetables, and olive oil. Served with crusty bread, it was a simple meal I could imagine sharing with St. Francis.

When we returned to our room, we discovered that our thoughtful host had left a small bottle of *vin santo*—sweet "holy wine" that, according to legend, was once used by a Franciscan friar to cure victims of the Black Death.

On the tray were two glasses and a small basket of diamond-shaped almond cookies, with a note attached: "For the Feast Day: the favorite of St. Francis."

We had seen these cookies at every bakery in Assisi that day and were told that Francis had loved this treat since childhood—so much so that he requested them on his deathbed as his final meal.

We took our glasses of holy wine and the basket of cookies up to the little rooftop deck. There we sat beneath a canopy of stars, dipping cookies in wine, feasting on the simple joy of being alive, and waiting for the full moon to rise above the horizon.

A ssisi had offered me the chaos of an unexpected festival and the calm of a hermit's cave, a chapel blessed with forgiveness, a ceiling of stars, and the loving embrace of two saints—a presence that reverberates through time and space.

I reflected on how, when a saint dies, it is their date of death that becomes a feast day—a holy remembrance of their return to Love.

And yet when my father died—a saint in my own life—that date became one of devastation and shattering. It was a rupture I hadn't been able to bless.

As I pondered my own grief and how it was evolving, I thought: What if this could be the beginning of, little by little, allowing Dad's death day to become not just a day of sorrow, but a quiet Feast Day?

A celebration of the life he lived and the light he brought to the world, even though it ended so abruptly and violently.

A time to honor the beauty of his life, his return to pure love, and the ways he still lives on in the unseen world.

What if Dad and Francis and Clare are sitting beside one another now, somewhere in the great field of eternity—talking to the birds, laughing at the old burdens they've finally laid down, being nothing but love... pure, glorious love.

@

Joy

In this complex
world where
grief hides beneath
everything that hurts
we only need
what is simple
what is true.
A single
teardrop
of forgiveness
to crack the
hardened heart
and release at last
unbridled
Joy.

NOVENA DAY 9

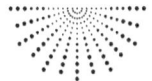

POMPEII - GARDEN OF THE FUGITIVES

It is through ... Radical Love that the bitter becomes sweet, the thorn turns into a rose, the pain contains healing, and the dead come to life.

— RUMI

We left Assisi early in the morning for a long but much-anticipated trip to Sorrento that involved three different trains with stops in Rome and Naples. The rolling hills and medieval towns of Umbria gave way to the coastal landscape and vibrant cities of Campania.

By the time we arrived, we were exhausted but grateful to return to the salt air and cool breeze of the coast.

Our hotel was cliffside on the southern edge of Sorrento, requiring a steep uphill walk and then an elevator ride up five floors just to reach the reception area. But the view was spectacular—from the terrace bar and restaurant we could see across the

Bay of Naples to Mount Vesuvius, resting majestically on the horizon as the sun set in full technicolor.

We enjoyed a huge dinner on the terrace—lasagna, fish, salad, potatoes, and a lemon cake that was a specialty of the house—as darkness fell and the stars and city lights began to flicker.

The next morning we set out to explore Sorrento. I was looking for a place for the final Novena prayer and wanted it to be awe-inspiring and also unexpected—perfect as the emotional and spiritual climax of this pilgrimage.

But I hadn't planned it in advance. I didn't want to feel the same disappointment I'd experienced in Assisi, so I decided to trust my intuition and Divine Guidance to show me the right place.

We saw a street that had been built 2,000 years ago and stone steps carved into the rocky cliffside that were even older than that. In the old town, we passed a community bulletin board that held death notices for neighbors who had recently died—a custom common in this region. We also learned that some older women still observe the traditional mourning practice of wearing black for three years after the death of a spouse or child.

I thought about how gracefully Italy makes space for public mourning and doesn't ask us to hide what is painful. That was one enormous gift of this entire trip for me—feeling supported in my grief, with no need to explain or justify my sorrow.

Strolling along the pedestrian-only shopping street lined with little stores, we noticed that lemons were everywhere. Markets sold lemons in a variety of sizes, shapes, and colors; there was lemon pasta, cookies, chocolates, perfume, and soap; and lemon-adorned pottery, towels, utensils, and aprons.

The climate here is perfect for growing several different kinds of lemons, much like we'd discovered in Monterosso al Mare. We tried a sample of limoncello—a lemon liqueur that is common in the region—with a strong bite of citrus and a sweet, smooth finish. I bought some to bring home, along with a jar of lemon marmalade, as a reminder of the bittersweet nature of grief and the joy that comes from embracing all of it.

E ventually we found a cathedral, and I had great hopes that I would discover exactly the right spot for this final Novena prayer. The church had beautiful interior doors and a display of the Stations of the Cross, all crafted in traditional local *intarsia* (inlaid wood).

There was a large nativity scene and a shrine to an older man who seemed to be from contemporary times: Dr. Giuseppe Moscati. I barely registered his name then, but I would recall it later when it was brought to my attention once again.

I walked outside, and my heart sank in disappointment. There had been no moment of inspiration—no statue, or painting, or chapel that called to me for the ninth prayer. I didn't want this final ritual to be an afterthought—I needed it to be meaningful for Julio's family and also a breakthrough moment for my own grief experience.

I realized I was asking for a lot—but it felt like the culmination of something sacred.

O ur hotel concierge had recommended spending the afternoon in Positano, just 45 minutes away by bus. We could sightsee there and take a scenic ferry ride back to Sorrento. It sounded fun—and I wondered if I might find the perfect

Novena prayer spot there. Maybe I was being guided to Positano for a reason. We had to leave right away.

What we didn't know was that the bus would travel a narrow, winding road with hairpin turns and no guardrails—veering precariously to the cliff's edge every time another bus or truck passed in the opposite direction.

Our eyes were wide with concern from the outset, but when the bus began making terrible screeching sounds, we moved beyond fear. The driver eventually pulled over as far off the road as possible without tumbling down the cliff and announced that the bus was broken. We would have to wait for another—outside.

Standing on the hot pavement, watching cars and trucks navigate precariously between our stalled bus and the stone cliff walls, I wondered if this had been a mistake—or perhaps a spectacular opening for the final Novena prayer.

I was trying to remain optimistic.

But in reality, by the time we finally arrived in Positano we had less than one hour before the last ferry of the day left for Sorrento. There was no time to find a church, so we sat on the beach with a glass of wine, immersed for just a moment in the beauty of the Amalfi Coast, with quaint Positano as our backdrop.

Another disappointment.

Another reminder that I needed to relax and let things unfold in their own time. That was the lesson I seemed to be learning over and over again. There had been many other reminders on this trip that I am not the one in control: missed trains, a stolen wallet, closed churches, unanticipated crowds.

And then there was the larger life lesson still unfolding: even when I thought I could control the H1N1 virus in our clinic and prevent tragedy, I did not actually have that power.

Like this trip to Positano, the road of loss and grief can be harrowing—full of unpredictable curves and breakdowns, with no certain destination or timeline. But somehow, we learn to make the most of the smallest moments of beauty and joy. And we find meaning in it all.

I would later come to understand that maybe the deepest healing doesn't come from holding everything together, but from letting it fall apart.

The next day we took the train from Sorrento to Pompeii—a place I had wanted to visit since reading about it in childhood. There was something magical about a city frozen in time by a natural disaster.

Pompeii has long been the subject of myth and legend, featured in countless works of literature, art, and film. We humans are drawn to explore such "lost cities" to better understand the past —and perhaps to glimpse real life interrupted by tragedy.

We fear death, yet are magnetically drawn to it in places like Pompeii, where we can wander the ruins and also explore what has been buried within ourselves. I hadn't known when I planned this part of the trip that something in me had also been frozen for years, waiting in the ruins beneath the ash until the time was right for excavation.

Pompeii was a thriving city at the time of its destruction in 79 AD, according to the eyewitness account of Pliny the

Younger, who watched the eruption of Vesuvius from across the Bay of Naples at 1 p.m. on August 24 and later wrote about it.

The city was literally frozen in a single moment—buried under 30 feet of ash and pyroclastic flow, which caused roofs and floors to collapse, though many walls remained intact.

Most residents are thought to have fled when a threatening black cloud first appeared above Vesuvius that morning. But some stayed behind—perhaps unable to flee, or unwilling to believe it was necessary—thinking they would be safe indoors.

When an unusual umbrella cloud resembling an umbrella pine rose from Vesuvius, Pliny the Elder—an admiral in the Roman navy and uncle to his young namesake—had sailed toward the disaster in hopes of rescuing people. But he lost his own life in the attempt.

In his recounting of the tragedy Pliny the Younger lamented the death of his scholarly uncle—the author of *Natural History*, a book that influenced many Renaissance thinkers including artists and architects and even poets, like Dante.

Walking the stone streets of Pompeii's shopping district felt eerily similar to wandering through the Old Town of Sorrento. There was a fish and produce market, marked by frescoes still visible on the walls; a kind of ancient "food court," with a counter holding large openings for pots of hot food sold for takeaway; and various shops, bath houses, and brothels.

The needs of day-to-day human existence haven't changed all that much over time.

F rom everything we can see today and glean from artifacts, Pompeii must have been an incredibly vibrant and beautiful city, its buildings covered in white ground-marble stucco, nestled in the fertile hills at the base of Mt. Vesuvius.

Pliny the Younger described Pompeii as "the most living of dead cities," and there is still an aliveness there—a sense of possibility hanging in the air, like a song interrupted mid-verse.

But the most haunting aspect of Pompeii is the plaster casts of those who remained behind in their beloved city. In 1863, archaeologists found pockets of lower density in the petrified ash. They poured liquid plaster inside, which solidified and formed casts of the victims, whose bodies had decomposed inside their fossilized tombs.

Several were on display in glass cases in the Fish and Produce Market—the fear and anguish still tangible in those frozen shapes, arms raised in protection, knees drawn up in defense.

Later, near the end of our tour, we visited the Garden of the Fugitives, where 13 more bodies were found in 1961—adults and children fleeing the eruption, caught in a vineyard and outdoor dining space.

My heart broke when I recognized that one of the figures was a woman lying on her side, looking down at a child curled toward her. I was overcome with emotion, imagining the helplessness and terror of that moment—especially the mother, desperate to protect her child from harm.

It was a vision that shattered something deep within me: like Mary holding the body of Jesus, like Catherine burying the plague victims she could not save, like Julio's mother cradling his lifeless body in the emergency room—this mother and child, immortalized in ash and earth, uncovered again what I had long buried.

I sat in front of those plaster casts—hollow inside like sealed-off memories, like grief frozen into form, like all that is too painful to speak—and I wept.

I finally released the tears that had been frozen inside me since the death of my father. Through sobs, I spoke the final Novena prayer over this sculpture of mother and child—a *pietà* of ash and stone to end the journey, just as Michelangelo's *Pietà* had initiated it.

The Divine Feminine held me and my grief, and held all the wild grief of life in her sacred, unbreakable arms.

"May this nine-day pilgrimage of grief through Italy somehow bring peace and solace to Julio's mother—may she, too, find her own way to carry the pain of extraordinary loss."

And I continued to sit there, holding in my heart that mother and child who had died 2000 years ago in a disaster no one could prevent, no one could change, no one could fix.

I saw clearly: even the deepest love cannot prevent death.

We simply cannot change the fact that we are mortal. We will all die eventually. It has always been that way on this planet—and always will be. It is a law of the universe: even stars ... and planets ... and galaxies will ultimately die.

No one has the power to stop death. That fact cannot be changed.

But it can be carried—with wisdom.

We can witness death in all its forms as part of the cycle of life, surrender our illusions of control, and cherish each moment more deeply, even while grieving what has already slipped away —and what is inevitable in the next breath.

Like those souls at rest in the Garden of the Fugitives, we may try to flee—to outrun death—but that is not in our power. Disaster and tragedy will arrive with or without our consent.

We cannot know all the answers, but healing does not arise from knowing.

It thrives on sacred witnessing ... and surrender.

The last day of our travels brought us to the chaotic, raw, endlessly fascinating city of Naples. One of the oldest cities in the world, Naples has experienced countless triumphs and tragedies over its long history of wars, conquests, natural disasters, and decline.

But this hectic, noisy, dirty city has a gritty resilience that comes from being tested by heartbreak—it wraps itself in a grief-shroud and embraces life wholeheartedly, even while living with the constant threat of Vesuvius looming nearby.

Death and life are intertwined in the winding narrow streets of old Naples: with laundry hanging overhead, death announcements posted on every corner, produce boxes stacked outside markets, motorcycles whizzing by, graffiti marking walls, mourning wreaths on doors, vendors hawking their wares, garbage bins overflowing, horns honking, people shouting.

This city is raw, uncomfortable—but as real as it gets. There is no pretense here—no fluff—just life spinning out of the strata, rising from the ashes, growing from the mud. Sorrow is palpable in the soul of this place—and mourning is welcomed into the city's open arms.

. . .

We visited the National Archaeological Museum, where artifacts from Pompeii and Herculaneum are housed and protected. These were the riches of the two buried cities that had lain in secrecy for centuries until explorers excavated and removed them.

Viewing these prized possessions of people who lived so long ago —accumulating material goods to create an illusion of permanence and purpose in this world—I was reminded again that everything we treasure, along with life itself, can be wiped away or buried in an instant.

There is no security. We have no control. Death and destruction have their way with us.

But life somehow manages to flourish in the wreckage of our attachments. It's a brutal reality—but beautiful too.

In the shadow of Vesuvius, with constant reminders of its devastation, there are certain gifts that can only be found in this challenging locale. The region is famous for San Marzano tomatoes—sweet, fleshy fruit with thin skin and a pointed oblong shape.

Prized for making flavorful sauces for pasta and pizza, these red gems grow only in the volcanic soil of this region, where high levels of phosphorus and potassium yield their sweet, rich flavor.

These rare tomatoes are so valued they carry their own stamp of certification from the government, which requires that they be allowed to ripen on the vine and be harvested by hand during the months of August and September.

They represent a form of "slow food" that Italy is famous for—the energy, time, and love invested in the production of such food is life-sustaining, transformative, and unlike any factory-farmed food available elsewhere.

Also uniquely grown in the rich soil of Vesuvius are the grapes used to make special "volcanic wine" such as *Lacryma Christi*—the tears of Christ—whose grapes were first harvested as long ago as the 5th century BCE by Greek farmers.

The secret of this special wine was eventually kept by Capuchin friars who settled in the area and continued to produce it in large quantities. The growing conditions here are tough for grapevines, whose roots must dig deep to find enough water and nutrients.

But the result is smaller grapes with compact and complex flavor that yield a smoky, earthy wine unlike the wines of any other region. In fact, it is said that the volcanic soil has a greater influence on the flavor profile of the wine than the variety of grape itself—Chardonnay grapes grown there will produce a wine that tastes unlike any other Chardonnay.

So the soul of this entire region has been shaped by Vesuvius and its looming, haunting form on the horizon—representing trauma, loss, fire, ash, depth, resilience, transformation, singularity, timelessness, uncertainty, impermanence, beauty, tenacity.

You can feel it in the air and taste the sulfur as you breathe in—with gratitude—for just one more moment of survival. Life is so fragile and precious here.

On the street corner, as we walked through the historic center of Naples, we saw a kiosk with a glass display case full of unusual pastries. We bought one to share and were told it was *sfogliatelle*, a shell-shaped pastry made with thin layers of dough that look like the pages of a book spreading apart.

The dough is crispy and flaky and melts in your mouth, and the filling inside consists of smooth, citrusy ricotta. Warm from the oven, this delectable treat was life-changing in that moment.

Another example of Italy's slow food, *sfogliatelle* is a true art form of this area and a strong symbol of Naples' culture and heritage—appearing in literature and songs as well as everyday life. But to us it was a reminder of the sweetness of just being alive—right here, right now.

We were just steps away from a church that had originally been a palace—Gesu Nuovo—and we decided to get out of the heat and noise of the city and take a quick tour, not knowing we would find one last moment of inspiration inside.

The interior of Gesu Nuovo Church was stunning, with ornate Baroque marble, frescoes, and statues. But a large bronze statue in a chapel to the right of the nave caught my eye.

I recognized the face as the man in the photo in Sorrento's cathedral: Dr. Giuseppe Moscati, whose tomb resided in the chapel before us. People were waiting in a long line to kiss the altar and then reach for the outstretched hand of the doctor, which had become highly polished over the years with thousands and thousands of touches.

It turns out that Moscati was a brilliant physician born in 1880 who had studied 20 different medical specialties in order to become the best diagnostician possible—in fact, he could accurately diagnose patients just by hearing their symptoms, without even examining them. His research led to the discovery of insulin.

He was also an extremely compassionate man who cared for the poor for free and sent them home with the medication they needed and some cash that he secretly slipped into the bag.

When Mount Vesuvius erupted again in 1906, he helped evacuate all the elderly and paralyzed patients from the hospital before the roof collapsed under the weight of the ash.

He was a third-order Franciscan, just like Margaret of Cortona and St. Francis himself—not ordained, but living by vows of poverty and service. When I read that Dr. Moscati believed in treating the whole person and that love had the power to heal, I felt I had met my mentor. I decided to wait in line with all the other pilgrims just to touch his hand.

After his death, people began to report miraculous healings that occurred when they prayed to this good doctor—and there is a room filled entirely with *ex-votos*: tiny red and silver plaques of gratitude for prayers answered with the help of Dr. Moscati. He was declared a saint in 1987 and is the patron saint of doctors, physicians, and those rejected by religious orders.

Here, across the world from the clinic where I first met Julio and his parents, I connected with a doctor who seemed to share a heart with me.

When I touched his hand, I asked once again for peace for Julio's family, and then a new prayer crossed my lips:

"Help me carry the guilt of a healer who cannot always heal."

I knew that Dr. Moscati had likely felt the same pain I was struggling with—the agony of being unable to help or save the most vulnerable person, even with the power of love. I later read an excerpt from a letter he wrote to the father of a girl who had died in his care.

He said that he kept a portrait of the girl on his desk along with fresh flowers, to remind him of "the frailty of human things. Beauty, every enchantment of life—it all comes to an end. **Only eternal Love endures.**"

I was inspired to write a letter to Julio's mother, following in the footsteps of Dr. Moscati. A letter I would never mail but that poured out my sorrow and let her know that I carried her and her son in my heart throughout Italy.

They will stay in my heart forever.

The entire cycle of Novena prayers felt complete by this touch of the good doctor's hand.

I had allowed my guilt and shame to come to the surface—for being a healer who couldn't create a miracle.

I felt love and compassion stir in my heart—for myself—the healing warmth, the reassurance that self-forgiveness would be possible someday.

That night we visited a restaurant where pizza was first created 100 years ago for our final meal of this journey—and in fact, pizza is the only food on the menu.

Our Margherita pizza arrived hot from the wood-fired oven—its chewy crust charred just the right amount, the buffalo mozzarella melting into the scarlet sauce of San Marzano tomatoes.

Each ingredient told a story. The tomatoes grown in volcanic soil, nourished by ash and time. The mozzarella, crafted from the milk of water buffalo raised on ancient pastures. The wine in my glass—a varietal shaped by hardship, forced to root itself deep in unyielding terrain, drawing minerals from the molten veins of Vesuvius.

This was no ordinary meal. It was the final step of the pilgrimage —a moment of closure, reflection, and gratitude.

I remember how I feared this entire trip was ruined as I waited at the airport to depart for Rome with a sick sense of doom inside. I worried that grief would overshadow everything.

But perhaps ruin was required—not as a destruction of what had been planned, but as an opening to what needed to heal.

The volcano erupts, the ashes fall, and the soil becomes more fertile than ever before.

The soul of this place has taught me: transformation is born of tragedy, of letting go, of waiting, of excavating.

Vesuvius gave me more than a lesson—it gave me a gift.

Its silent presence beneath every footstep, every breath, every stone of Pompeii reminded me that buried things are not lost forever.

Grief, when honored, ripens into wisdom.

Guilt, when faced, yields grace.

And healing is not a single linear path, but a long, slow spiral—one that I am finally ready to receive.

Healer's guilt transcends into love—the Divine picks up the pieces of the broken world without judgment.

Circle
We keep walking
this endless circle
through grief and guilt
trembling with fear
and uncertainty
never looking up
to see
stars suspended
in black sky
whose light flickered
four thousand years
before our
first breath.
How does such
mystery and miracle
unfold in every moment
without end?
Only through Love.
Only Love.

PART THREE

The Return

Bring
back
medicine
to heal
the
world

HOME AGAIN

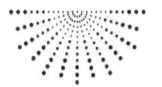

When you come out of the storm you won't be the same person who walked in. That's what the storm's all about.

— HARUKI MURAKAMI, *KAFKA ON THE SHORE*

Early the next morning, we arrived at the airport in Rome for our flight back home, and I was already dreading the transition. We stood in line for an hour waiting to check our bags, only to discover we were in the wrong line and our flight would soon be taking off.

When only two seats remained on the plane, a sweet young couple ahead of us offered to take a later flight so they could enjoy their honeymoon for one more day, leaving the last seats for us. But I wished more than anything that I was the one staying behind.

When I had boarded the flight to Rome just weeks before, I was venturing into unknown territory—filled with grief and certain that our trip would be completely ruined. I had no idea how I would survive the itinerary I had planned a year earlier, but I knew that I had to go.

I arrived in Italy devastated by sorrow and confused by the depth of pain I was experiencing. Only later did I realize that Julio's death, while tragic in itself, had also exposed a chasm of unexpressed grief and guilt from my past—hidden away for decades.

In the end, Italy was exactly the place I needed to be with my overwhelming grief. It had provided a safe container for me to explore my deepest pain.

What had once been the unknown was now intimately familiar. Somehow each city, each Novena prayer, every piece of art, each meal had become an integral part of my transformation.

I had walked through ruins and cathedrals, stumbled through train stations and terraced gardens, carried my prayers through narrow streets and hushed chapels. I had followed the scent of lemons, the footsteps of saints, the flowing of the waters.

And slowly, quietly, my travels through this land had opened something in me. I had discovered parts of myself I hadn't known before—and I didn't want to lose that.

Now, as our flight carried me closer and closer to home, I realized I was returning to an old familiar world as a completely new person. With each passing mile, I felt the sacredness of this pilgrimage slip through my fingers. I was leaving behind the safe crucible where my deepest grief had been revealed.

As the mystical aura of my travels dissolved, I came to terms with the fact that I had to return to the "real world" and face the aftermath of Julio's death.

.   .   .

I was relieved that I had two days to rest before my first shift at the clinic—the place where I had learned of Julio's death on that awful morning, where I had reassured his parents in my broken Spanish that he should recover from this flu without much difficulty, the place where I used to believe that my love for my patients had the power to heal them.

My tender heart was safe for just a bit longer—or so I thought.

On the way to our house, I stopped at the grocery store to replenish our food supply for the coming week. But a shock awaited me there: when I walked into the entryway, the first thing I saw was a large picture of Julio displayed on a table, with a request for donations to help his family pay for medical and funeral expenses.

I burst into tears at the sight of his sweet, innocent face in the photo—probably taken at school just weeks before he died.

I remembered the emergency travel cash stashed in the lining of my backpack and took all of it out—over $200 in bills of various denominations. I stuffed the money into the donation box while still sobbing. Every emotion of the pilgrimage surfaced and poured out in my tears, which flowed freely even though I was in a public place. I couldn't stop them.

But when I was done, I felt relieved—emptied of the remnants of uncertainty, shame, and doubt that had been tangled inside me.

That moment represented the true completion of my Healer's Journey. I had come full circle, returned home, and made my final offering to Julio's family. There was nothing more I could do except carry on as best I could in this real and painful world.

. . .

Back at home, as I unpacked my bags, I arranged the red-beaded rosary on my little altar—a circle of comfort and remembrance that had traveled with me for the entire pilgrimage. I placed a medallion of St. Catherine holding a lily in the center of the coiled rosary. These were powerful symbols of the holding and acceptance I had found for my grief throughout my travels in Italy.

On the shelf above my writing desk, I stacked books about St. Catherine and Dr. Giuseppe Moscati, my two mentors—both healers who practiced love and yet still couldn't save everyone. I silently asked for their support for the day I would return to the clinic, and I felt, for a moment, that I was not alone.

Sometimes the entire Universe reaches out for those who bring love to the world—and cushions the landing when things fall apart.

When I finally returned to the clinic a few days later it seemed as though I had never left. The hum of a busy medical practice was unchanged from before: with patients chatting in the waiting room; front desk clerks typing on keyboards and answering incessantly ringing telephones; clinic assistants rushing to check in patients, find lab results, schedule appointments; doctors and PA's dictating notes while hurrying from room to room.

It was all exactly as I had left it. But *I* was different. I stood back and noticed how my energy and pace didn't seem to fit in this scenario. And I was afraid to admit that my heart didn't really want to be there.

The CEO of the clinic invited me out for a glass of wine after work that day and wanted to know about the trip. When I tried to find the words to explain the mystical journey I had under-taken—the depths of grief I had explored, the way things had unfolded and fallen together perfectly even when they seemed to be ruined and broken—my words stumbled and I struggled to tell her even the most basic details of what happened. She seemed disappointed with my travel story, wanting to hear about art and vineyards and romantic moonlit strolls.

"Why were you feeling grief?" she asked, incredulous. "It wasn't your fault the boy died. His parents didn't take him to the emergency room soon enough."

She told me the clinic had moved on from Julio's death while I had been away. I was fascinated to think that while I was in the midst of a daily deep exploration of grief and guilt as a medical provider, my "home base"—my office support team—had simply put the whole thing behind them.

We had been living in totally different worlds for those weeks I was away. No wonder it felt like I didn't belong there anymore. I couldn't explain how the death of a patient in our clinic had unlocked repressed grief and guilt from 20 years earlier and plunged me into a mystical journey of the soul. It made no sense to her—or to anyone I knew in the ordinary world.

I asked how Julio's family was doing and she told me they had initially been extremely angry and were interviewed on the local news, blaming our clinic for Julio's death. But after a week or so something shifted and their anger had dissipated for some reason. They were working through their sorrow quietly and had expressed a small amount of gratitude for the care Julio had received.

I felt a sting of guilt once again—the revelation that they had delayed taking Julio to the ER crushed me. I knew they didn't feel safe going to the ER—they couldn't afford the expensive care and they didn't know how to navigate our complex medical system.

That was the entire reason we had created this low-cost clinic—to remove financial and social barriers to care for families like Julio's. Once again, love hadn't been enough to fix everything in this situation.

Now I understood more fully the burden of guilt and grief being carried by Julio's parents—who would surely have done anything to prevent their son's death if it had been possible—if they had known—if they had seen the future—if they had been able to control the universe.

I was deeply familiar with that pain of the unknowable and the unthinkable. Now all of the prayers whispered across Italy seemed even more important.

Our pain had connected us across the planet.

I couldn't tell the CEO about the Novena I had conducted for this grieving family or that I had prayed for my own broken heart, which she seemed unable to comprehend. I felt like a visitor from another planet, speaking a language that no one could understand.

This isolation in my own home environment felt worse than the day I arrived as a stranger in Italy carrying my bags full of grief. I had to repress some of the pain again in order to return to my job. I had to lock some of the doors once more to keep my sanity in a place that no longer felt like home.

But even though I had to temporarily hide my pain again, something was very different this time. Julio's death had given me a key to those deep chambers that stored my grief—and my guilt, as well. The guilt of a healer who cannot save those she loves along with all the other shame that comes from being an imperfect human.

My travels in Siena and Cortona had helped me see the layers of guilt that I had been protecting for so long. I didn't fully understand how they had become so stuck but I finally had an inkling that I needed to focus my healing work on that. Of course that turned out to be anther journey that would take far longer to navigate. But it was the beginning of my spiritual transformation.

During the months after my return from Italy I felt an urge to tell the story—to write this very book. But I didn't have the words then—or the insights and the bigger vision that time affords. Some tales can only be told in retrospect after a long season of reflection and growth.

And sometimes still more shifts are needed—more travels, more risks, more strangers and saints, and more falling apart.

In my case I would meet a woman with special gifts shortly after my return who conveyed a mysterious message to me that came to her from the unknown: there was another path for me to follow and it was time for me to shift my career. Intuitively I resonated with her words—this is what I had recognized on that first day back at the clinic.

The pilgrimage had transformed me and made a different path possible—even mandatory. I would end up retiring from clinical medicine a few months after my return from the "ruined trip" to start a new journey: writing books.

And that has brought me to this place today where I record this story of mysticism, miracles, magic and the mundane—a wild and holy path through grief, guilt and grace to deeper love and expanded consciousness.

I haven't yet learned everything that a lifetime can teach about death and grief and guilt. But I have gained some tools for navigating the journey. I see now that all the losses of life have shaped me—not just by wearing down my rough edges or cracking open my deepest hidden chambers, but also by becoming part of the very fiber of my being.

When we carry loss and grief openly, without apology or shame, they integrate into our physical existence—bones and blood, cells and senses, organs and atoms.

We become the embodiment of Love with all its sorrows and joys woven together for the brief magnificent spark that is our lifetime.

This I believe is why we are here—to become Love incarnate for the few precious moments that are granted to us.

To harvest all the wisdom available to us through our losses.

To shine with the light of the stardust that forms us.

To weep and laugh in the same breath.

To finally allow all that is impermanent to dissolve away … as we return to pure Love.

EPILOGUE

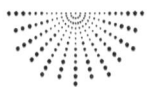

Grief is itself a medicine.

— WILLIAM COWPER

The journey I have described in this book took place several years ago and because it changed my life I recognized that I should write about it one day. Over the years I tried to start writing this book many times, but after every attempt failed, I began to believe I couldn't do it. The words just wouldn't come and I concluded that maybe it wasn't an important story to tell after all.

Then I received an unexpected, unexplained diagnosis: congestive heart failure with an enlarged right atrium and abnormal rhythm.

How could it be that my heart—the source of my strength, my courage, my love—was failing? How was it possible that I had always been so healthy, until one day everything fell apart?

In my distress and confusion, I felt called to explore my heart from every dimension—not just physically, but emotionally, spiritually, and energetically as well. I began journaling, writing letters to my heart, and listening for her response. Through somatic therapy, I uncovered buried layers of anger, grief, and guilt that had long remained hidden.

I heard a podcast interview with Francis Weller, the author of *The Wild Edge of Sorrow*, where he described how grief literally gets stuck in the heart and "congests" it energetically.

Grief and guilt kept coming up for me again and again.

Could it be that the "old" grief from my father's death that I had re-explored on the trip to Italy was somehow still affecting my heart?

As I sat with all the insights that were becoming clear to me, I heard the message: **You must write.**

I had feared that my medical condition might mean I would be too frail to ever write again—but this guidance told me the opposite: WRITE. NOW.

Everything pointed me back to the pilgrimage of grief and guilt through Italy, years earlier—the story I had failed to tell many times before. So I pulled out my old journals, notes, and unfinished pages and began, slowly, to retrace my footsteps on that remarkable journey.

I continued tending to my heart each day: rising at dawn to journal, reading mystical texts, dancing and boxing to release rage, practicing self-forgiveness, walking barefoot on grass and sand, and holding my precious grandbabies as they slept on my chest.

In my search for a new perspective on my health I reimagined my diagnosis as an "expanding" heart rather than a failing one, inspired by a verse from St. Teresa of Avila:

> *"The soul is filled with a peace so deep that it feels as if its heart were being widened, stretched open by love, to receive more than it ever thought it could hold."*

With each paragraph I wrote, I felt a little stronger. Slowly, joy and vitality began to return. My opened heart was holding more love than I ever imagined possible.

What I didn't know then—what I could not have predicted—was that something even more astonishing was still to come.

After living with a disrupted rhythm for eighteen months, my heart spontaneously returned to sinus rhythm just after I completed the first draft of this book.

No procedure. No medication. Just rhythm. Just breath. Just grace.

I don't have an explanation. But I believe this book—its grief, its love, its truth—was part of the medicine.

I realized then that I was continuing the spiritual pilgrimage I had begun on that so-called "ruined" trip to Italy. Revisiting each stop helped me recognize the deep archaeology of grief that had always been there.

Italy's ruins—layered with centuries of sorrow and tears—had held my own grief and guilt too. And I had found them there, beneath the surface of stone and prayer.

Writing this book became another Novena: an act of mourning, excavation, and healing.

I understand now that the journey will never be finished. There will always be more to learn—and deeper ruins to explore.

Over the years, I had reflected on the remarkable journey through Italy many times. When I would see the rosary on my little altar, coiled around the St. Catherine medallion, I would remember Mary's face in the *Pietà*. When I opened the books by Catherine and Dr. Moscati, I found I was still touched by their words—and by their healing hands reaching across time to comfort me.

The deeper lessons that had unfolded on that journey were now clearer to me—from the moment I sat down to plan our perfect itinerary for Italy to the day I encountered the donation box for Julio's family in the grocery store. It was as if the entire experience had been orchestrated by a Divine travel agent, responsible for the trajectory of my spiritual healing and evolution.

I thought I could control everything with my detailed trip itinerary and the "pandemic plan" I created for our office. I thought I could bend nature to my will and prevent anything "bad" from happening—that I had the power to guarantee no patient would die of the H1N1 flu (or anything else) before our trip to Italy. I was going to create the perfect trip, no matter what it took.

But circumstances lined up against me from the beginning—though I now see they were actually in service of my growth.

I was called in on a day off to see Julio, who never would have been my patient—or triggered my eruption of grief and guilt—if a staff member hadn't been taken ill that day.

When I stopped at the clinic for just one moment as we were leaving for the airport, it happened to be the very moment the ER called to report Julio's death. Without that precise timing, I wouldn't have learned of his death until we returned from Italy.

And many synchronicities occurred during the trip, as if an unseen map was guiding it:

-Getting lost in Rome and retreating to the old church where a mysterious hooded monk was waiting with a prayer request basket ...

-Wandering into the cathedral in Trastevere at the exact moment a funeral was taking place ...

-Visiting the Jewish Ghetto during Rosh Hashanah festivities ...

-Witnessing the annual Palio celebration dinner in Siena ...

-Finding the olive tree sculptures in Cortona that mirrored the ancient "walking tree" we had seen ...

-Arriving in Assisi on the Feast Day of St. Francis.

These events unfolded within the itinerary I had created a year earlier, but they far exceeded the original vision I had for the trip. I thought I had planned a perfect romantic sightseeing vacation in Italy—one that had been ruined by the untimely death of my patient.

But in the end, the itinerary was perfect in its own way, as a pilgrimage of grief ... a journey I desperately needed to take, but had not recognized or planned.

. . .

The Universe is fascinating that way—sometimes our path is aligning one step at a time, and we simply cannot see it.

We think we've failed.

We think everything is ruined.

But often, it's in those liminal moments—those unravelings and detours—that the path is most poignant, most aligned with our growth, most essential for our transformation.

And yet, it's the hardest time to see clearly.

The only thing we can do in those moments is find the courage to take the next step.

And even if we don't yet understand where the path is leading, we walk on—because something sacred is unfolding beneath our feet.

@

What I came to understand—only years later—is that my grief in Italy was much deeper than "healer's grief" over the death of a patient. Julio's death had opened the sealed chamber of sorrow I'd carried since my father's suicide, where guilt had frozen grief into something heavy and unyielding, particularly because it was complicated, traumatic grief that I didn't know how to carry.

Francis Weller writes that suicide tears a hole in the psychic foundation that can take decades to mend. It certainly did for me.

I once believed that grief was the suffering I needed to escape. But I've come to see that grief is the medicine. It is guilt—not grief—that blocks transformation. When guilt is softened through forgiveness, grief can flow again, like a wild river of love.

That's what Italy gave me. A path through the ice. A return to love. And the beginning of a spiritual transformation.

@

The Novena turned out to be a profound practice, inspired serendipitously at that little church in Rome. One of the reasons it helped with my grief was that it provided a grounding, sacred ritual space each day where I could revisit my pain and sorrow.

Though I didn't see it at the time, there were layers of revelation and recognition woven into these nine Novena stories—and the lessons they've continued to unfold throughout this ongoing journey.

The prayers and the steps that led to them were acts of mourning—making grief visible through words and movement and presence:

At the **Vatican**, I was awakened to the power of the Divine Feminine to hold grief and sorrow, and to witness our suffering. There is more Love for you in the Universe than you can imagine —asking for help makes it visible.

In **Trastevere**, at a stranger's funeral, I connected with the need for community in our grief and mourning rituals. Grief becomes an integral part of life when we share the pain and carry it together.

Florence revealed enduring historical and ancestral grief, resonating through art, science, and poetry. Even the greatest tragedy can lead to Renaissance, rebirth, and fertile soil. Grief is a key to transformation.

On **Grazie Bridge** I learned the value of gratitude—not just for life's blessings, but for loss, longing, and living in the not-yet and the not-known. Grief for the dark times of life is the bridge to joy.

In **Monterosso**, I discovered the power of Nature to soothe and support us through the impermanence of life. Nature is a healing balm and carries grief in its DNA, as do we.

Siena revealed the deep subterranean layers of grief, where both guilt and grace can be excavated—if we do the necessary work. It taught me to reinterpret the darkness as a time of opening, retrieving, soothing, and shining light into the hidden recesses.

Cortona allowed all of my guilt—a lifetime of it—to become visible, available for reflection and healing. Guilt is ultimately an exiled part of the self that can be embraced and transformed by forgiveness to become pure Love.

In **Assisi**, I received a gift of forgiveness before I even realized I needed it, in the divine light of St. Francis. I was reminded to stay present, release control, and accept what life is offering in this moment.

Finally, in **Pompeii**, the circle was complete—like a rosary—with a return to the Divine Feminine in the ashes. And in Naples, with the touch of a doctor who healed with love and tempered guilt with grace.

Through these nine Novena prayers, I was given a map to uncover the archaeology of my grief and the guilt that buried it—and also the tools to meet each challenge along the way.

I will never cease walking this path—and that's okay. There will be more losses to grieve, more guilt to unearth from the ruins. But now I have an inkling of how to do it, and a few more tools to use.

I have learned to be patient and allow the path to unfold with its own timing—9 prayers, 9 months, 90 years, 900 lifetimes—whatever it takes.

This is how we must change the world:

We carry our own grief and use it to transform suffering into joy and deep presence.

We forgive whatever was forgotten, undone, or broken long ago —because to continue regretting it will destroy us.

We celebrate the darkness that allows us to recognize the light.

We dance in the ashes of loss, knowing they will nurture what has yet to be born.

We toast our departed with holy wine under the stars—grateful for each moment we shared together.

On this journey through Italy I discovered that you don't have to be religious to pray ... or to find solace in ancient churches ... or to ask the Divine Mother for help carrying the pain.

You don't have to be an expert in art history to see grief in a brushstroke or a carved figure or a sculpted tree.

You don't have to be a scientist to be awed by the colors of the setting sun or the way an olive tree holds its dead timber in its arms as it endures for centuries.

In this time of "selfie tourists" who visit sacred sites as backdrops for social media posts, I was called to be a *grief tourist*— exploring with reverence the hidden corners of subterranean ruins, whispering prayers in dark chapels, climbing rocky paths, weeping over plaster casts, tossing flowers off ancient bridges.

I descended to the depths of Italy only to discover my own heart there—wild and holy with grief ... and the guilt of a healer who cannot save everyone.

I do not fully understand Grace but I know that it arrived without being summoned, and stayed even when I doubted it.

Grace was present in the missed turns, the unexpected encounters, the unraveling and remaking of my heart. It met me in stone churches and crowded trains, in grief-stricken prayers and unexpected laughter.

And perhaps this is the truest evidence of Grace: that somewhere along this winding, holy path, I found my father again. Not as I had remembered him in the shadow of trauma and guilt, but as he truly was—in his coveralls and work boots, standing quietly among the saints, with his humble nod and gentle smile. Simply present. Human and holy all at once.

Grace invited me to this journey and accompanied me every step of the way. But grief has been the portal for every transformation:

For every lesson learned

For every wound healed

For every particle of light that illuminates my path

For every pulse of love that radiates through me.

Grief—touched by Grace—has changed everything ... and made it holy.

And now, as I lay this story down, my heart beats in rhythm again.

Not because the grief is gone—but because I walked through it.

Grace met me in the ruins.

And rhythm returned.

APPENDIX

TOOLS FOR THE GRIEF JOURNEY

This life is built almost entirely of love and losing, isn't it?

— ANDREA GIBSON

This book has traced my path through grief, guilt, and grace, but this journey is not mine alone.

The following nine-day ritual is offered as a guide for those carrying unspoken grief or hidden guilt. You might choose to practice it over nine days, or take each day as it comes, in your own time. You'll find reflections, simple practices, and short prayers designed to help you on this journey into the darkness to retrieve the light.

Begin wherever you are, with whatever you have, and consider using a journal to reflect each day. May love carry you the rest of the way.

A Personal Novena for Healing and Release

Day 1 – Create a Sanctuary for Your Grief

Establish a sacred space for your ritual. This might be a small table, corner of a room, or outdoor setting. Include objects that feel grounding or meaningful: photos, a candle, a smooth stone, a journal, dried flowers—whatever gets you in touch with your grief.

Ritual: Build an altar or "grief corner" and return to it each day, even briefly. Light a candle if it feels right.

Prayer:

Guide me through this journey. Let me feel held as I remember what has been lost. Let this space be a container for sorrow and love.

Day 2 – Mourn What Has Been Lost

Acknowledge the people, places, relationships, or dreams that have ended—those named and unnamed. Include collective losses as well: climate grief, injustice, mass death, ancestral suffering.

Ritual: Bring a flower to a memorial site, or release petals into flowing water. Name the losses aloud or in writing.

Prayer:

Bring peace to all who carry grief alongside me. Let my mourning join the great river of remembrance that flows through time.

Day 3 – Look to the Sky: Grief Is a Cosmic Law

Lift your gaze. Let the sky, stars, or vastness above remind you that grief is not solitary or out of place—it is part of the cosmology of love.

Ritual: Watch the stars. Light a lantern. Recite the names of your ancestors. Lay under the sky and weep.

Prayer:

Heal me, and heal those who came before me. Let this grief be a ripple of love stretching across generations.

Day 4 – Practice the Five Gratitudes

Gratitude and grief are twins. They arrive together, aching and holy. Reflect on five things you're grateful for—especially those that feel tangled with loss.

Ritual: Journal your responses to these:

1 Life

2 Love

3 Laughter

4 Loss

5 Longing

Prayer:

Let gratitude arise even in darkness. Help me embody thankfulness as a companion to my sorrow, and share it gently with others.

Day 5 – Connect with the Healing Power of Nature

Let the natural world support your nervous system. Let trees, stones, water, and sky absorb what you can't carry alone.

Ritual: Walk barefoot. Hug a tree. Watch the sun set. Sit with your back to a stone wall. Rest under the sky and let the wind speak.

Prayer:

Infuse every cell and atom of my being with your calm, life-giving presence. Let me call upon you when the world feels too heavy.

Day 6 – Gaze into the Shadow

Turn toward what you've hidden—the shame, the pain, the broken places that have not yet been seen or named. Meet them in the soft light of love, not judgment.

Ritual: Sit in silence with a journal. Write what you're afraid to speak. Light a candle in the dark.

Prayer:

Illuminate the places I've buried. Let your light reach into my shadow and show me what still longs to be held.

Day 7 – Face the Voice of Guilt with Compassion

If guilt arises—whether rational or not—let it surface. Hold it with kindness. You are not here to punish yourself. You are here to heal.

Ritual: Write your guilt on a piece of paper, then tear or burn it. Or release a leaf or flower into flowing water with the words: I release you.

Prayer:

Grant me the courage to release self-blame. Let guilt be alchemized into love, and love into action.

Day 8 – Practice Radical Forgiveness

Let go of how your mind says it should have been. Forgive what cannot be changed. Offer the same mercy to yourself that you would to someone you love.

Ritual: Practice Ho'oponopono for yourself:

I'm sorry. Please forgive me. I love you. Thank you.

Prayer:

Let forgiveness rise like water over stone. Let me receive my own tenderness with open hands.

Day 9 – Return with Love

You are not the same person who began this ritual. Let your grief become a blessing for the world. Let your transformation ripple outward.

Ritual: Write a blessing from your new self to the self who began this journey. Keep it on your altar. Read it aloud.

Prayer:

Let me carry this love-soaked grief into the world as a quiet offering. May it bless those I meet. May it continue the healing.

Healer's Grief

In the course of this journey, I've often reflected on the hidden burdens carried by those who care for the suffering and the dying. Physicians, nurses, chaplains, social workers, and so many others are often deeply affected by the losses they witness day after day. This sorrow has been called healer's grief — the cumulative weight of tending others while rarely having space to tend our own hearts.

Because I know many of you who read this book may also serve in these roles, I've included here a set of resources and practices we created to support healers in acknowledging and working with their grief. My hope is that these offerings will remind you that your pain, too, deserves a place at the table of remembrance and healing.

Mindset: Making Space for Death Within Life

One of the most important shifts we can make on the journey of healing guilt is to change the way we see death itself.

In modern times, we have been taught — often without even realizing it — to see death as a mistake, a failure, something unnatural.

When death is seen as something "wrong," then every loss becomes a personal defeat. Every sorrow becomes a place where we believe we should have fought harder, saved more, prevented the inevitable.

And guilt, born of love and helplessness, roots itself deeply in our hearts.

But death is not out of order.

Death is part of life's sacred, ancient rhythm — as natural as the falling of leaves in autumn, the setting of the sun, the return of the tide to the shore.

When we allow death to take its rightful place within the cycle of life, something begins to soften inside us.

Guilt, once buried in the shadows of "I should have done more," can emerge into the light. It can be seen for what it truly is:

— an expression of love,

— a longing for more time,

— a sorrow that we could not stop the turning of the great wheel of life.

When guilt is bathed in that light, it no longer needs to punish us.

It can become part of the great love that connects us — to those we have lost, and to the sacred mystery that holds us all.

Meditation: Allowing Death to Take Its Place

Purpose:

To soften the heart's resistance to death, and to invite death back into the sacred circle of life, where guilt can dissolve into compassion.

Preparation:

- Find a quiet place where you can sit or lie comfortably.
- Close your eyes if you wish.
- Place one hand over your heart, and one hand lightly over your belly.

The Practice:

1. Breathe with the rhythm of life

Inhale slowly: *"Life."*

Exhale slowly: *"Death."*

Inhale again: *"Birth."*

Exhale: *"Return."*

Let your breath rise and fall like the ocean — a continuous cycle, ancient and unbroken.

2. Visualize the Great Wheel

- Imagine a great wheel turning gently in the sky above you.
- Upon its rim are the seasons: birth, growth, decline, death, and renewal.
- See that death is not an end point, but part of the sacred circle — always leading toward new life.

3. Offer a Silent Blessing to Death

Whisper inwardly:

"You are not my enemy. You are my teacher, my companion, my necessary return."

4. Release the Guilt Into the Circle

- Imagine the guilt you carry — the heavy burdens of "I should have..." or "If only I had..." — as small stones in your hands.
- Offer them to the turning wheel.
- Watch as the wheel gathers them, softens them, weaves

them into the soil of life, where love and sorrow become new seeds.

5. Close with a Breath of Mercy

- **Inhale**: *"I am part of the cycle."*
- **Exhale**: *"I am forgiven."*

Sit quietly for a few moments longer, feeling yourself held in the great rhythm of existence.

NOTES:

This meditation can be practiced anytime guilt feels heavy or when grief feels stuck. Over time, it gently reshapes the heart's relationship to loss.

Self-Forgiveness Practice:
Walking with What You Could Not Control

Introduction

We often carry guilt for what we could not control — whether as caregivers, healers, or grieving loved ones. True self-forgiveness is not about denying responsibility, but about releasing ourselves from impossible expectations and recognizing our shared humanity.

This practice invites you to walk gently with what you carry, and to offer yourself the mercy you have long withheld.

Step 1: Ground Yourself in the Present

Find a place where you can stand or walk slowly. If possible, go barefoot on grass, earth, or stone. Feel the ground beneath you.

Take several deep breaths, exhaling slowly. Place a hand on your heart or belly.

Step 2: Speak What You Carry Aloud or Silently

Bring to mind a specific guilt or burden you've carried.

Say or whisper these words:

"I have carried the weight of believing I should have done more.

I have carried the pain of not being able to change what happened.

I have carried blame that no one asked me to hold."

Step 3: Place the Burden in Imaginary Hands

Visualize placing that burden in the open hands of life — whether you picture God, the earth, a wise ancestor, or simply the air around you.

Say or whisper:

"This is too heavy for me to carry alone.

I offer it back to the mystery, where all things are held in love."

Step 4: Bless Yourself with Compassion

Place your hands gently over your heart and speak these words:

"I forgive myself for not being perfect.

I forgive myself for being human.

I forgive myself for carrying more than I was ever meant to hold.

I am worthy of compassion. I am worthy of release. I am worthy of love."

Step 5: Close with Gratitude

Take one more slow, deep breath and offer thanks — not because it's easy, but because you have taken a step toward freedom.

You might end with:

"I walk forward now, not free of memory,

but free of blame."

Mini Release Practice: A Moment of Grace

Purpose:

For the times when guilt or sorrow rises unexpectedly, and you need a quick, simple way to offer yourself compassion.

The Practice:

1. Pause and Place a Hand on Your Heart

Wherever you are — standing, sitting, walking — pause for just a breath.

Place your hand gently over your heart.

2. Breath in Compassion, Breathe Out Release

Inhale slowly: *I did the best I could*

Exhale slowly: *I release what was never mine to carry.*

(Or use you own words if they arise.)

3. Visualize Light

Imagine a soft, warm light — like a candle or the sun — filling the space where guilt was sitting.

See that light spreading through your chest, your body, your spirit.

4. Bless Yourself

Whisper quietly (or in your heart): *I forgive myself. I am forgiven. I am free.*

5. Continue Your Day

Carry that small light with you, even if it flickers.

NOTES:

This practice can be done anywhere—at a bedside, in a hospital hallway, on a walk, lying awake at night. You can repeat it as many times as needed. Over time it becomes a habit of choosing mercy over blame

Pocket Prayer: When Guilt Rises

Life breathes in, death breathes out.
I am part of the turning wheel.
I release what was never mine to hold.
I forgive the one who tried.
I belong to the sacred rhythm of life and return.

Reflection for Healthcare Providers:

The Stillness That Holds Everything

You are always moving.
From room to room. From crisis to comfort.
From decision to decision, without a pause.

And yet — there is stillness, even here.

Not at the edge of your day, but at the center of it.
Stillness is not a luxury you must earn.
It is a presence that holds the pulse of everything you do.

It is in the space between heartbeats.
In the moment before the diagnosis is spoken.
In the breath you forget you are taking.

Stillness is not absence. It is anchor.
It is what lets you return to yourself,
without needing to leave the work you do.

Today, you do not need to find stillness.
You only need to notice it — already waiting,
within the breath, the silence, the moment between tasks.

And when you notice it, even briefly,
you return to the part of yourself
that has not been depleted by giving.

The part that is whole.
The part that is held.
The part that is still.

Micro-Practice: A Threshold Mantra for
Returning to Presence

In a life of constant motion, stillness doesn't need time — it needs intention. One way to invite stillness into a busy clinical day is through a simple threshold ritual: a quiet mantra repeated in the moment just before you enter the next room, answer the next call, or begin the next task.

It's a way to:

- release the last interaction,
- gather yourself into the present, and
- step forward with clarity and care.

Step 1: Choose a Sacred Pause

Pick a small moment that repeats throughout your day:

- When your hand touches a doorknob
- When you walk through a hallway
- When you press "enter" on your keyboard
- When you take off or put on gloves

This is your personal threshold.

Step 2: Create a Simple Mantra

Something quiet, grounding, and meaningful to you.

It might be:

"Let me enter with light."

"This is the only moment."

"Leave the last. Meet the now."

"Presence, compassion, breath."

"Nothing is mine to fix. Only to hold."

Or something entirely your own.

Keep it short enough to say with a breath — no more than a line or two.

Step 3: Repeat as Needed

Each time you reach your threshold moment, silently speak your mantra.

Let it reset your nervous system, even for one breath.

Let it become your doorway back to yourself.

This practice requires no extra time, no change in workflow.

But over time, it becomes a string of tiny still points in your day — moments when you are not just functioning, but returning.

Not every moment will be peaceful.

But every moment can be entered with presence.

And that is how stillness walks beside you — even here.

Final Reflection

I resonate with the exiled—
the ones misunderstood in their time
but who kept creating anyway.
With St. Francis,
who spoke the language of birds and stars
and signed his name with a Tau.
With those who poured their grief into fresco and clay,
who brought heaven to earth
through the work of their hands.
With the healers who gave everything
to tend the torn and discarded,
who kept loving
even when it was impossible to save everyone.
With the ones who sometimes felt lost or weary
but never extinguished the little light within.

I am one of them.
And so are you.

This is my final offering.
Not from a fragment, but from the whole of me.
The girl who burned her poems.
The woman who returned for her.
The soul that now speaks with all its voices.

May you find the light within you—
even the smallest ember—
and know it has always been
enough.

ACKNOWLEDGMENTS

This book was carried by many unseen hands. I am grateful to the artists and visionaries of Italy whose work spoke across centuries, to the teachers of suffering who revealed its hidden gifts, and to the companions of spirit—both living and departed —who walked with me in silence. Above all, I am thankful for the readers who now take this journey into their own hearts, completing the circle of grief and grace.

Reader's Discussion Guide

This guide is designed for readers, book clubs, and circles of friends who want to reflect more deeply on the themes of Wild and Holy. Use the questions for group discussion or as personal journaling prompts. There are no right or wrong answers—only honest reflections from your own journey.

Discussion Questions

1. The book begins with a sudden loss that reshapes the author's planned trip. Have you ever had a life event disrupt your plans in a way that led to unexpected meaning?
2. Wild and Holy explores the tension between grief and guilt. How have these two emotions shown up together— or separately—in your own experience?
3. The author describes her travels as a kind of "pilgrimage." What does pilgrimage mean to you? Can ordinary travel —or even daily life—become a pilgrimage?
4. Works of art and architecture play a powerful role in the book. Was there one image, story, or place that particularly resonated with you? Why?
5. The book names grief as both wild and holy. What do these two words mean to you when you think about loss?
6. The journey is described as a kind of "Novena"—a ritual of nine days. Do you have rituals (religious or personal) that help you move through grief?
7. The author experiences a "second wave" of grief decades after her father's death. Have you ever revisited old grief long after you thought it was healed?
8. Pilgrimage often involves both descent and return.

Where in your life do you feel you are descending?
Where do you sense you are returning?

9. In what ways does the natural beauty and history of a place—like Italy in this story—affect your inner life? Can landscapes themselves become teachers?

10. After finishing the book, what insights or practices do you want to carry with you? How might grief itself become a companion or teacher in your own life?

Closing Reflection

Take a few minutes to write or share: If you could create your own "grief pilgrimage," where would you go, and what would you hope to find there?

ALSO BY KAREN WYATT MD

7 Lessons for Living from the Dying

Award-winning book sharing wisdom learned from hospice patients about love, forgiveness, and living with purpose.

The Journey from Ego to Soul

A guide to spiritual growth that explores how grief and mortality help us transcend the ego and live from the soul.

The Tao of Death

A contemplative adaptation of the Tao Te Ching, offering 81 verses of guidance for living and dying with peace.

Stories from the Dark Night

Reflections on grief and creativity as pathways through life's darkest passages.

Conversations on Death with ChatGPT

Explorations of mortality and meaning in dialogue with emerging AI.

For more books, reflections, and podcast conversations, visit www.eoluniversity.com.

ABOUT THE AUTHOR

Dr. Karen Wyatt is a hospice physician, spiritual teacher, and the bestselling author of *7 Lessons for Living from the Dying*, a book of profound insights drawn from her work with patients at the end of life. Her other titles include *The Journey from Ego to Soul*, *Stories from the Dark Night*, and *The Tao of Death*. She hosts the *End-of-Life University Podcast*, featuring conversations with leaders in the field of death and dying. Known for integrating spiritual wisdom with clinical experience, Dr. Wyatt teaches that embracing mortality is essential for living a meaningful life. Her work invites us to transform grief, illness, and impermanence into gateways for awakening.

Invitation to Connect

Thank you for joining me on this wild and holy journey. My hope is that these pages have been a companion for your own path through grief, love, and meaning. Writing this book has been both a pilgrimage and a prayer, and I am honored that you have walked alongside me.

If you would like to continue the conversation, I invite you to stay connected:

Listen to my podcast **End-of-Life University** at eolupodcast.com for interviews and reflections about death, dying, and the lessons of life.

Visit my website eoluniversity.com where you'll find resources, articles, and information about my other books.

Subscribe to **Soulcode,** my Substack newsletter at karenwy attmd.substack.com where I write about grief, spirituality, and the evolving relationship between humanity and technology.

Most of all, I hope you will carry forward what this book has stirred within you. May you find beauty even in sorrow, grace within brokenness, and healing in the most unexpected places.

With gratitude,

Karen